Poppy Parade

Arthur Marshall was
Christ Church, Camb
housemaster at Oundle
the Second World War
an Intelligence officer, later at Combined Operations, and then SHAEF. He was Lord Rothschild's private secretary before becoming a full-time journalist and broadcaster in 1964. He has written several books, including *Whimpering in the Rhododendrons* (1982) and his autobiography, *Life's Rich Pageant* (1984), both available in Fontana.

Poppy Parade

Humorous anecdotes of
service life collected by
Arthur Marshall
for The Royal British Legion

Fontana/Collins

First published in 1985 by Fontana Paperbacks,
8 Grafton Street, London W1X 3LA

Set in Linotron Plantin
Made and printed in Great Britain by
William Collins, Sons & Co. Ltd, Glasgow

Contents

Foreword

by General Sir Patrick Howard-Dobson,
National President of The Royal British Legion

As National President I am delighted to introduce this book of stories which is being published in aid of The Royal British Legion's Poppy Appeal in this fortieth anniversary year of the end of the Second World War.

Our thanks are due especially to Arthur Marshall who kindly undertook the vast chore of writing to potential contributors; to those same contributors, not least the Royal ones, who I believe have provided a book which will give delight to many; and to the staff of the Legion's publicity department, who have collated and coordinated, revised and reminded, and are very largely responsible for the remarkable fact that a bright idea has become a reality.

Thanks are also due to the publishers Hodder & Stoughton, Weidenfeld & Nicolson and Michael Joseph for kindly waiving payments.

Lastly, our thanks to everyone who buys this book. The work of the Legion grows no less; the fact is that anyone who was twenty on VE Day or VJ Day is sixty today – if he was thirty, he is seventy, if he was forty he is eighty. We shall be facing some very real welfare problems in the next ten years or so and your contribution will help to solve them.

I do hope that you will enjoy the book, and then persuade your friends to buy it.

Introduction
by Arthur Marshall

The British race may or may not be superior to all others, and 'may' is my own patriotic estimation, but in one respect at least it is unique. It has the ability to laugh at itself.

Other races have their own admirable characteristics but the above ability is seldom one of them. The witty and highly civilized French rarely turn their critical guns on themselves. The Germans (and I refer only to those who are within reach, so to speak) are merry laughers but solely at the world in general. The Scandinavians (can it be true that they have the highest suicide rate?) are full of charm but seem to the casual visitor to take everything rather seriously. Who can doubt that the Siberian salt-mines await any Russian who dares to find, and it would be quite a search, any of the USSR amusing? The Americans, perhaps the most generous race on earth, come nearest to us, but then, after all, we invented them.

The armed services would seem on the face of it to be the least productive seed-bed of humour, and abroad and in foreign services this is doubtless the case. But not here. Oh dear me, no!

Requests for comical anecdotes and merry reminiscences have brought forth a fine crop of fun. The range is wide, from the Chaplain of the Fleet's suspected brush with God and a jolly legpull by the Duke of Edinburgh, to an assortment of cheeky back-answers given by sentries (a favourite topic down the years) to persons of high rank. There has been humour to be found everywhere, even in such unpromising and serious undertakings as the Normandy landings, the disastrous Norwegian campaign of 1940, Dunkirk, the Malta convoys and even the yomping episode in the Falklands. There are lesser matters – a WRNS rating getting almost literally into a twist with her suspender belt, popular Irish jokes, Monty giving them what for in Moscow, and pleasantries voicing doubts about the intelligence of the Royal Marines (another favourite subject).

I was in the army for seven years, from 1939 to 1945, and although there were of course some dicey moments, my main memory is, happily, that of laughter. I am glad to find that I was not alone.

Nautical Nonsense

The Venerable N. D. Jones
Chaplain of the Fleet

During my early years as a naval chaplain I experienced the embarrassment of missing my ship. When I arrived at a small port in the Far East, the ship had sailed!

After considerable panic on my part, and lots of assistance from the local harbour office, signals reached the ship that the chaplain was returning and would be lowered on to the ship from a naval helicopter.

The dramatic moment came when, after sighting the ship and then hovering over it, I was winched down to the deck. Assembled there were fire parties dressed in their asbestos suits, and a number of others whose duties would be to receive safely any visitor.

As I ducked out of the area of the whirring helicopter blades, one of the group – a leading seaman – said, "'Ello, Vicar. Been having a word with the Guvnor?'

HRH The Duke of Edinburgh

The war against Japan was over. A task force consisting of *USS Missouri*, flagship of Admiral 'Bull' Hallsey, with four escorting destroyers, and *HMS Duke of York*, flagship of Admiral Sir Bruce Fraser, with two British destroyers, *HMS Wager* and *HMS Whelp*, was making its peaceful way towards Japan to receive the Japanese surrender.

It occurred to the captain of one of the British destroyers that the ceremonies would most probably involve representatives of the nations which had been fighting the Japanese. It also struck him that it might be quite difficult for some nations to get suitable representatives to Tokyo in time.

The evil thought then struck him that, as his doctor was Canadian, a Surgeon Lieutenant RCNVR, this might be a splendid opportunity for a legpull. He considered that the chances of the Canadians having a senior officer anywhere near Japan seemed reasonably remote and, as the doctor was unlikely to know the whereabouts of any of his countrymen who might be in the Pacific Ocean area anyway, the captain set about putting his plan into effect.

He proceeded to draft a general signal purporting to come from the Commander-in-Chief inviting the ships in company to report the names and ranks of any Canadian officers borne, knowing full well that apart from his doctor there were not any. This message was then suitably written out on a signal form and delivered to the unsuspecting doctor. The effect was immediate. The doctor pounded up to the bridge clutching the signal in a frenzy of anxiety about what it might mean. He protested to the captain that to the best of his recollection he had done nothing to bring himself to the attention of the C-in-C. The captain assured him that there must be some other reason and suggested the possibility that the C-in-C was looking for someone to sign the surrender document on behalf of Canada. The doctor was naturally rather tickled by this, but began to get a bit suspicious at the barely concealed sniggering of some of the bridge staff who were in on the joke. It was eventually conceded to be a legpull, to the merriment of all concerned.

In due course the doctor went about his business and the captain retired to his sea cabin. Time passed and all was quiet. Some hours later the 'buzzer' sounded in the captain's sea cabin and the voice of the officer of the watch was heard to say that a signal had just arrived from the C-in-C which he felt sure the captain would like to see at once. With that a signalman knocked at the door and delivered the signal to the captain. He could hardly believe his eyes when he read that the ships in

14

company were to report the names and ranks of any Canadian officers borne.

Having convinced himself that *his* leg was not being pulled this time, the captain desperately thought how he might best convince the doctor that this signal really was genuine. In the end he decided to send for the ship's Bible and the ship's doctor in that order. When the doctor arrived the captain placed his hand on the Bible and handed the signal to the doctor, swearing as he did so that this time the signal really had come from the C-in-C.

Sadly, as it turned out, a Canadian officer, senior in rank to the Surgeon Lieutenant RCNVR, was found just in time to sign the surrender document on behalf of Canada, but at least the doctor was invited on board *USS Missouri* to witness the ceremony. When it was all over he returned to his ship in the proud possession of an expended flash bulb used to record the ceremony. The historic bulb was duly mounted on a plinth and triumphantly displayed on the wardroom mantelpiece.

HRH The Prince of Wales

When I was flying helicopters in the Royal Navy I served for a period of time in *HMS Hermes*. She was then a commando carrier and, as such, was full of Royal Marines and their heavy equipment wherever it was necessary. During exercises I was always intrigued to discover that large numbers of marines used to queue up outside my helicopter, presumably hoping to be transported in my aircraft. I used fondly to imagine that they had instinctively recognized my talents as a pilot, until it was eventually revealed to me that the reason for my apparent popularity was that they thought my helicopter was better maintained than everyone else's and, therefore, less likely to plummet into the sea! The bootneck is a crafty character!

Vice-Admiral Sir John Woodward
Deputy Chief of Defence Staff

Firstly, I would warn anyone never to write in their diary, as I did in early March 1982, ' . . . life is fairly dull these days, it seems that admirals aren't allowed to do very much other than grace exercises, social and sporting events . . . '

*

I joined my first submarine as a very junior lieutenant of very little account with some trepidation and was duly surprised and a bit flattered when the busy, voluble and press-on first lieutenant/second-in-command called me 'Colonel' from the time of first introduction. This soon developed into a habit which I quite enjoyed in an unthinking sort of way. However, it all ended after some six weeks or so, when the first lieutenant approached me rather furtively to mutter, 'Colonel, I really can't go on calling you Colonel, what the hell is your name?'

Perhaps this accounts for *Private Eye* calling me 'Sir Sandy Whatsisname'.

Admiral Sir John Fieldhouse
Former First Sea Lord and Chief of Naval Staff

The commodore of the barracks at Chatham many years ago had been ignored by the gate sentry as he entered his establishment in plain clothes. From his office, he telephoned the officer of the day, who in turn telephoned the regulating petty officer, who in his turn stomped off down to the gate and asked the sentry, 'Have you seen the commodore?' The sentry said, 'No, RPO,' so the RPO phoned the OOD who phoned the commodore and told him that the gate sentry had definitely *not* seen him pass through.

The commodore thought he'd sort this out once and for all and went in person (again) to the gate.

He addressed the sentry: 'Do you know who I am?'

The sentry replied, 'No, mate.'

'I'm the commodore.'

The sentry, unabashed, said, 'In that case, mate, I'd push off if I was you – there's an angry RPO out looking for you.'

*

A junior seaman standing his first ever watch at sea was detailed off by the leading hand of the watch to be lookout. He was told to go to the starboard wing of the bridge, find his predecessor and get a turnover from him.

Our intrepid youngster groped his way in the darkness to the bridge wing, and said, 'Anybody there?'

A voice anyone else on board would have recognized as the captain's said, 'Yes, of course.'

But our sailor, not recognizing his captain's voice, said, 'Well, I'm your relief, so push off then.'

*

A young naval lieutenant and his lady attended the summer ball at *HMS Dolphin*. Afterwards, of course, he drove her to her home which was some miles away in a country village. Whilst returning from the village he began to feel tired. In those days before the breathalizer, one could be prosecuted for being 'drunk in charge', even, he recalled, in a parked car if seated in the driver's seat. He therefore pulled into a lay-by, got out of the driver's seat after removing the key, and stretched out in the back seat for a well-deserved sleep, still, of course, in his full uniform.

He was awoken minutes later, it seemed, by the law, in the form of a policeman shining a torch into his face.

'What might you be doing 'ere?' said the law.

'Well, officer, to be absolutely honest, I think I might have drunk too much earlier this evening, and in order to recover fully I have pulled into this lay-by for a short nap. You will note,' he added, 'that I have my car keys with me, and I am not sitting in the driver's seat, so I am sure you would not accuse me of being "drunk in charge".'

'An excellent plan, sir, and you would have been absolutely right,' replied the officer, 'only trouble is, though, this ain't no lay-by, it's a T-junction that you've parked in.'

Admiral Sir William Staveley
First Sea Lord

Every year, in November, each of the services is required to contribute to a number of loosely associated ceremonial occasions culminating in the Remembrance Day parade at the Cenotaph. From a naval point of view, the participants assemble some weeks beforehand at *HMS Excellent*. *HMS Excellent*, once the Royal Navy Gunnery School, is still the centre of ceremonial training for the Royal Navy. The parade staff, greatly diminished in numbers these days but nonetheless always able to lend a colourful turn of phrase to the occasion, take in a great variety of people – men and women, officers and ratings – to be trained for what is colloquially known as the 'November Ceremonies'.

Many people become involved, in one way or another, in the training for this series of important occasions, but, formally, the executive officer – known as the Commander of the Island – has no part to play first thing on Fridays when those under training on 'the Island' attend training divisions. He takes an interest, nevertheless.

On such an occasion, the Commander of the Island was observing the platoons of trainees marching past the saluting base, most of whom were being sent round for the fourth and fifth time for some imperfection of their drill. As a platoon of WRNS ratings marched away from the parade, anticipating another flood of invective from the Chief of the Parade, his attention was distracted by one young and particularly nice-looking lady. It was not simply that she reminded him of his granddaughter either; it was the odd lack of rhythm of her marching as she struggled to clutch something around her right thigh.

'You there!' barked the Chief of the Parade. 'You in the second from rear section of the WRNS platoon with the problem with your marching: what on earth is the matter with you? Report to me!' he shouted.

Puce with embarrassment, the young lady broke ranks – under the very critical eye of the commander by this stage – and made a somewhat undignified approach to the Chief of the Parade.

'What is the matter with you?' he reiterated. 'You got something wrong with your health?'

'No, Chief,' she said. 'It's my suspender belt; it's broken!'

Keenly aware of his audience, the Chief of the Parade was not

19

slow to catch the mood of the occasion.

'Never mind,' he said. 'Report to the commander. He knows all about that sort of thing!'

She didn't: she ran off overcome by embarrassment. But the commander had some difficulty in keeping a straight face.

Surgeon Rear-Admiral
S. G. Rainsford

The year was 1923. I was then serving in the smallest ship in the Royal Navy, namely *HMS Robin*. The *Robin* was one of five gunboats that patrolled the Si Kiany River and its delta known as the Pearl River, protecting shipping from piracy, etc. At the top of the delta is situated the City of Canton which has quite a large harbour. To the northeast side of the harbour lies the European Concession on a small island named Shamun, which is connected to the City of Canton by a number of small short bridges. The Concession was the home of a number of foreign consulates, namely British, French, Swedish but no German, since the Germans had been expelled from the Concession after the 'Great War'. It also contained the European Club.

In the middle of Canton Harbour is a large island. I have forgotten its name. It is completely built over and a number of very high, many-storeyed buildings on it can be clearly seen from the harbour. I became intrigued by this island, especially so since I learnt that it was seldom visited by Europeans, and, furthermore, that they were not encouraged to do so although it was only a ten-minute journey by motor boat from Shamun.

HMS Robin usually tied up to a buoy a few yards off the 'land' of Shamun and, early one morning, using one of *Robin*'s boats, I landed on this other island.

It is difficult without a guide to find your way about a Chinese city because of the narrowness of the streets. I soon became completely lost. I began to worry as to how I could find my way back to the landing stage where I was to be picked up by one of *Robin*'s boats and returned to the ship. After wandering about rather aimlessly, I suddenly came upon a wide open space, in the middle of which to my utter astonishment was a modern European-type of bungalow.

It was surrounded by a very pretty garden, a well-kept grass lawn and all fenced in by a low wooden fence. I was so intrigued that I began a closer inspection, when a young man aged about thirty appeared. He was tall, over six feet tall, very slim, of athletic build but perhaps a bit on the thin side. He had short blond hair, bright blue eyes, was clean shaven with a very pale complexion. I think you will agree when you have heard the rest of this story that his whole appearance made what happened both surprising and unexpected.

He enquired in English with a slight foreign accent whether he could be of any assistance. I explained who I was and that I was lost. He invited me into his house where some Chinese servants served us with some green Chinese tea.

I found out that he had been an officer in the German Army and had been forced to retire after the defeat of Germany in the Great War. He was now the representative of a German firm that manufactured diesel engines for the many launches that operated up and down the river. He had a very high opinion of the British Navy and offered to guide me back to the landing stage. I invited him to visit my ship and the European Club in Shamun. At first he was most reluctant, and told me he had never visited Shamun since the Germans had been expelled. However, after some persuasion he agreed to accept my invitation.

One evening, a few days later, we sent a boat to the island to collect him, and proceeded first to Shamun where we visited the European Club. The members of this club were always pleased to see us and it was quite easy to give way to too much

21

hospitality. For example, often one would find four or even five gins lined up in front of you on the bar without knowing who had ordered them. Our German guest was obviously embarrassed at first by all this hospitality but later thawed out. However, he refused to drink anything except beer – for every small gin that we downed he accompanied us by drinking half a pint of beer. After consuming a few drinks we returned to our ship for dinner. While waiting for dinner to be served, my captain and I had a cocktail and our guest another glass of beer.

At dinner we had some wine, but again our guest refused to drink anything but beer. I began to wonder how much beer a man could drink.

Before it was time for our guest to return home, my captain and I had a final drink and our guest a last glass of beer.

My captain ordered a boat to take him back to his island, and as he was about to board it and say goodbye I said, 'We don't know your name.'

He drew himself up to his full height and standing at attention he said in a most formal manner, 'I am a Prussian, an officer in the Prussian Guard, and my name is Von Beer-Shifter!' (Phonetic spelling of course!)

Commandant Patricia Swallow
Director, WRNS

Saluting

1. All WRNS Ratings must salute a WRNS Officer.

2. The saluting must be done with the hand. This is effected by bringing the said member of the Rating's anatomy smartly, yet with infinite grace, up to the brow, just to the end of the last but one hair of the eyebrow. Care must be taken not to violate the neutrality of the hairs either before, or

the one after, the regulation hair.

3. WRNS Ratings must endeavour to cultivate an extra sense in conjunction with the senses of hearing, tasting and smelling in order that they may be able to detect the advent of the 'chosen' before she appears. Thus, a perfectly timed and perfectly finished salutation will be rendered by the time the said 'chosen one' has passed out of sight. It is considered advisable for those desiring to become efficient in this art to practise in front of their mirrors for half an hour before breakfast every morning, and in addition, they should have in their possession a timepiece having a second hand, in order to evince both rhythm and poetry of motion.

4. Owing to the natural shyness and retiring nature of women Ratings we have, after due consideration, decided that there is no necessity for the saluting of RN, RNR and RNVR Officers.

(An extract from a mock Admiralty Order from the First World War)

Lieutenant-General M. C. L. Wilkins
Commandant General Royal Marines

A middle-aged man, frustrated by his lack of success in life, decided that the time had come for drastic action. He therefore made an appointment to consult one of the country's leading neurosurgeons, a man who had made his name in the relatively new but highly successful field of brain transplantation.

After some discussion with the surgeon, it was agreed that the patient should be given a new brain. The surgeon then offered him a selection. The first brain, which had belonged to a brilliant statesman and author, who had died tragically young, was priced at £20,000. The next, that of a Nobel prize-winner in physics who had also met an early death, was available for a mere £30,000. The surgeon then showed his patient what he described as the finest bargain available: the brain of a recently deceased colonel in the Royal Marines, which would cost his patient a mere £50,000. The patient, knowing little of the services, expressed surprise that a colonel's brain should cost so much more than that of a brilliant statesman or a Nobel prize-winner. 'Ah,' said the neurosurgeon, 'the unique advantage of the Royal Marine colonel's brain is that it is virtually unused.'

Lieutenant-General
Sir Steuart Pringle
Former Commandant General Royal Marines

There was this Irish secret agent who was going to be parachuted behind enemy lines on a clandestine mission.

When drawing his stores, he was issued with a main parachute, a reserve parachute and a folding bicycle. 'This is going to be a water jump,' he said, 'I don't need the folding bicycle.'

'Fine,' said the storeman, 'if you prefer to walk to the aircraft.'

*

The Irish secret agent was standing in the door of the aircraft with his two parachutes and folding bicycle.

'Red on,' shouted the Dispatcher, 'stand in the door . . .
Green on, go.

'Dispatcher to front gunner, when a chap on a bicycle
arrives, send him back here, over.'

*

The Irish secret agent pulled the ripcord of his main parachute
as he fell from the aircraft: nothing happened.

He pulled the ripcord on his reserve parachute: nothing
happened.

'I bet that when I get down,' he thought, 'the folding bicycle
won't work either.'

The Right Honourable
Nicholas Winterton
Member of Parliament

A new recruit on putting to sea and suffering with sickness said,
afterwards, that for the first day he was afraid he would die, and
for the second day he was afraid he wouldn't.

*

The Duke of Wellington, while reviewing his troops before
Waterloo, is reputed to have said, 'I don't know what effect
these men may have on the enemy, but by God, they frighten
me!'

Admiral of the Fleet
Sir Edward Ashmore

In early 1947, in the winter, Field-Marshal Montgomery came to Moscow to receive his Order of Suvorov from Stalin. As the lowest form of animal life at the British Embassy, namely interpreter for the naval attache, I was lucky to be in his entourage for his visit to the Kremlin.

It was a bright morning, thirty degrees of frost, thick snow and no wind. We came into the Great Square of the Kremlin and paused before the great gun. General Slavin, Commander of the Moscow Garrison, was conducting the Field-Marshal who quite reasonably asked if it had ever been fired. I do not remember the answer because Monty's attention quickly switched to the cathedrals which border on the square, beautiful in the morning sun with their domes shining. 'I would very much like to go into those,' said the Field-Marshal.

'I am sorry,' said Slavin, 'they are under repair.'

'How very interesting,' said Monty, 'I am so glad to hear that you are looking after your cathedrals and would be delighted to see the work that is going on.'

There was a hurried consultation after which Slavin said, 'I am very sorry, Field-Marshal, but today is a special day, you are here, and they are all locked.'

'That is all right,' said the Field-Marshal. 'Get the key.' And someone was sent off.

We were stamping our feet a bit by now; it was very, very cold. Some ten minutes later the man came back and spoke to Slavin, who looked extremely worried, turned to Monty and said, 'I am very sorry Field-Marshal, but we seem to have lost the key.'

'I see,' said Monty. 'All right, I will stay here until you find it.' Find it they did and in we went. In terms of how the Soviets ran things in those days it was no small victory!

*

I took over command of *HMS Alert* in 1953 in the wake of an unusual experience of my predecessor.

One of the Chinese members of the ship's company, when she left Hong Kong to come south, had been arrested by the Customs who seized a certain amount of gold in dust and bars on board. On the way south, ship's officers had decided that they could make a better search of the ship than the Hong Kong Customs and had a go. They found nothing. But twenty-four hours out from Singapore the 'makee-learn' on the wardroom staff asked the first lieutenant to come into the pantry with him. There stood the usual covered cheese dish, and he lifted the cover. Underneath, instead of a bar of mouse-trap, there was a bar of gold. The first lieutenant took the hint and the officers searched the ship again. This time they found quantities of the stuff on top of ventilators, in odd corners; all the places they had looked before. So, the finds went into the captain's safe and a signal was sent to the Customs, who came off and searched the ship again in the Singapore Roads (cutting to ribbons in the process the lining of the Commander-in-Chief's wife's fur coat, which I fear did not help matters as far as my predecessor was concerned). But they found nothing more and the ship proceeded to naval base. At least one of the ship's Chinese, no doubt in fear of his life, never left the ship during her stay.

We applied boldly for a reward for the ship's company's efforts in having averted the smuggling of some hundreds of thousands of pounds' worth of bullion. But this, I was told, was no more than their duty. I often wonder what the outcome might have been if the gold had still been in my safe and the ship's agent's aid enlisted. But it was ashore 'for safe keeping'; we never saw it again and never knew what caused the Chinese change of heart. The Treasury profited for sure!

*

My wife and I had a Chinese gentleman called Ah Sang who looked after us in our bungalow in Singapore, which, having been condemned as unfit for European occupation some years before by the rubber company which owned it, had been lived in by naval officers ever since. He taught us something about Chinese loyalty and enterprise.

On one occasion my wife offered our admiral some of our banana trees for his new garden and then she came to Hong Kong with me in my ship. The delighted admiral wrote to us there to say how pleased he was with our banana trees. When we came back the garden looked the same. 'Oh yes,' said Ah Sang, 'the Admiral's *gabun* (gardener) came but I didn't want to spoil our garden so I sent him to Captain W's *gabun*, he has splendid banana trees.' I do not think Captain W ever knew.

As a reward, Ah Sang asked for a new stove. We thought the present one was perfectly adequate and he was very crestfallen. Some two weeks later he came to my wife and said, 'Mem, come and see my new stove,' and sure enough there was a perfectly shiny article in the kitchen.

'How did you get that?' she asked.

'Oh,' said Ah Sang, 'my friend gave it to me. He asked for a new stove and he has an easier Mem.'

*

In the early days of the British Pacific Fleet *HMS Swiftsure*, wearing the flag of Admiral Brind who then commanded its cruiser squadron, went north from Sydney to make the first contact with the fifth fleet, and Admiral Spraunzs.

My signals team had to contend with a series of flashing lights on each entry into the harbour – the kind of unofficial use of signalling which was heavily frowned upon in the Royal Navy. I remember 'Welcome from the signal gang of *USS Colombia*' at Manus, and among the greetings at Ulithi, 'Hello *Swiftsure*, where is the other half of the British Fleet?' Once at sea, on exchanging identities with one cruiser, back they came with 'Aren't you rather new?' Indeed we were. This reached the admiral who made back, 'Aren't you rather fresh?' Without, I know, any but the nicest intention. My poor staff spent the next quarter of an hour, as the ships drew further apart, taking down the most effusive apology.

*

During the Norwegian Campaign in 1940, *HMS Jupiter*, in which I was Sublieutenant and so navigation and boarding officer, was patrolling the Leads south of Vestfjord. One morning, I was sent in the whaler under oars to board a Norwegian merchant ship. Having scrambled up the rope ladder clutching, mentally at least, my pistol in one hand and the cards provided to help with the language in the other, I was of course received in the most friendly way by the master, who spoke excellent English.

He was kindness itself and I came down the ladder again, proudly equipped with a splendid set of navigation charts of the area. These were a navigator's dream, right up to date, with all the sectors of the lights, which were sometimes on in those days, in colour. They were to be a great help in subsequent patrols when, as you rounded a corner, every beacon on a rock looked at first like a submarine periscope.

In some euphoria I settled down in the stern-sheets as we pulled back to the ship. Some minutes later . . . 'Excuse me, sir,' said my very young signalman, Olver.

'Oh yes, what is it?'

'Excuse me, sir, but is the plug meant to be out?'

We put it back and stayed afloat. No wonder I specialized in signals!

*

We came into the Grand Harbour in Malta early one morning in June 1942 after a bad passage in which four of our six ships in convoy were sunk and another mined on the way in. We lost a number of escorts in the operation, including the hunt-class destroyers ahead and astern of our ship, *Middleton*, as we made the final approach through a newly mined channel. As we entered harbour thousands of Maltese clustered and gathered to cheer us in. It was just the welcome we needed and made up for the only berth available to us being the ammunition wharf.

As another air raid began, and we prepared to cast off, a *dghaisa* came alongside, and a young Maltese in it sprang up the gangway. 'Any wardroom laundry please, sir?' It was a nice return to reality. But we sailed before dark through the wreck-strewn harbour, both sorry and still soiled.

Sir John Harvey-Jones
Chairman, ICI

I was one of those who started his naval education at Dartmouth before the war, where a strong sense of ceremonial was engendered in all of us. I was therefore particularly proud as the senior snotty of a wartime 'D' class cruiser to be given the task of collecting the British ambassador in Uruguay with the captain's motorboat, which I was responsible for driving. Unfortunately, for it was in the early days of the war, we had just returned from an extensive search of some three months for a German raider lost in the South Atlantic and had failed to realize the effects on some of our equipment.

We set off in fine fettle: boat's crew in No. 1s, myself wearing my dirk, the Royal Marine band and guard of honour on the quarterdeck ready to welcome the distinguished visitor. However, the seams of the boat had opened and we were making water fast. When about half way to collect the ambassador, in plumed hat and full regalia, it dawned on me we could neither make it ashore nor back to the ship. A rather tatty boat's crew and bedraggled midshipman eventually swam ashore at the steps and established a new, fortunately not too frequently repeated, ceremonial drill.

Major-General Julian Thompson
Major-General, Royal Marines,
Training Reserve and Special Forces

The Royal Marines Mountain and Arctic Warfare Cadre trains the instructors in mountain and arctic warfare techniques for the Royal Marines. The war role of the cadre is as the brigade reconnaissance troop for 3 Commando Brigade Royal Marines, directly under the command of the brigade commander.

The final exercise for the budding instructors (corporals and sergeants) in March 1982 was a new one designed by the officer commanding the cadre. Part of it involved a march from the north to the south of the Mull of Kintyre. At the post-exercise debrief on 1 April 1982 one of the corporals said, 'The long "yomp" down the Mull of Kintyre was unnecessary and far too long. Nobody these days carries that much kit, for that distance, over that type of terrain on foot.'

The following day Argentina invaded the Falkland Islands. The corporal and the remainder of the course went to war with their erstwhile instructors in their war role.

In Port Stanley on 14 June 1982, the same corporal was asked if long 'yomps' were necessary in training. He declined to answer!

Colonel J. Hughes
Former Chairman of the Poppy Appeal

Smudger was a rather unsophisticated young able seaman on messenger duty. Called to the admiral's office, he was told to take a despatch to a destroyer anchored amid stream. Rather naively he asked the admiral, 'But how will I get out to the ship, sir?'

'Take out my pinnace,' thundered the admiral in exasperation. And that's how Smudger first learned that a pinnace was a boat!

*

At an inter-services rugby tournament the navy were playing the army. A young lady in the stand inquired of the young officer escorting her, 'Why do the army always wear red jerseys?'

'So that the blood won't show when they're injured,' said her boyfriend.

A crusty old admiral sitting behind them added, 'Yes, my dear – quite true – and that's why we in the Royal Navy always wear blue jerseys!'

Admiral of the Fleet
The Lord Hill-Norton
Former First Sea Lord and Chief of Defence Staff

The catering officer in a pre-war destroyer's wardroom had a hard time. His mess mates were always moaning about the food; not enough, too fancy, so dull, always the same, and so on and so on, day after day.

Fed up with this, and having built up a useful balance in the mess fund, the caterer decided to surprise them. He went ashore and bought a huge bowl of beluga caviar to serve for lunch on Sunday.

Came the day; really fresh toast, slices of lemon, thin brown bread and butter were ceremonially handed round by the mess waiter. The caterer himself bore in one of the silver rose bowls, just about full of this delicious stuff, and ceremonially handed it round. Taking some himself, last of course, he sat down and waited for the applause.

The first lieutenant, keeping his head, was the first to speak, as follows: 'Oh gawd, not eggs on toast again.'

*

A midshipman in the fleet flagship, engaged on a project for his journal, sought and obtained permission to go down a coal mine on a 'make and mend' day, while his ship was visiting the Firth of Forth.

He went ashore in uniform, made his way to the mine, changed into the appropriate kit and spent a happy afternoon at the coalface. When he had had enough he came up, bathed and changed at the pithead, and set off to return to his ship.

He had not gone far when he met one of his senior officers who had been playing golf, and asked the young man to take his clubs back to his ship.

By chance, as he approached the gangway, he saw the Commander-in-Chief walking the quarterdeck, so he spruced himself up, put the golf clubs as neatly as he could over his shoulder and mounted the gangway.

The admiral, noted for his quick temper and a poor opinion of the modern young officer, returned our hero's salute and said (rather to his surprise), 'Well, my boy, had a good round?'

'No, sir,' replied the snotty, 'I've actually been down a coal mine.'

He spent the next twelve hours at the masthead, clutching the golf clubs.

Major Ewen Southby Tailyour
Officer Commanding 539 Assault Squadron Royal Marines

In 1971 I was the officer commanding the Royal Marines detachment in *HMS Fearless* and my MOA (marine officer's attendant, or batman in army parlance) was a quite outstanding marine named Underwood. He had served for years at sea, loved his job, was always immaculate and was a stickler for insisting that 'his' officer was attended to in the manner that he, Underwood, believed to be correct. He also believed that the service he gave should not be affected by the daily inconvenience of life at sea.

Thus it was that on a certain day in September, as the ship steamed north from the Shetlands, the embarked admiral decided to hold his annual Operational Readiness Inspection. Amongst other drills the ship was made ready for the worst that modern warfare could throw at her. This included the securing of the officers' cabins for action, a lengthy process by which everything inflammable or moveable was stowed away, bunks were folded up, shaving mirrors were taped over, drawers were sealed shut, curtains and carpets removed, and the hand basin was filled with a gallon of water for dousing small fires. The entire ship's company, including the admiral, was required to wear action working dress and to carry antiflash gear, respirators and lifejackets.

As the long line of inspecting officers concertinaed to a halt along the passage adjacent to the officers' cabins, I was horrified to see the reason from my position at the very rear. The curtain of my cabin was swinging out into our path as the ship rolled

34

gently. I guessed the worst and as I crept up past my fellow inspectors I was in time to hear the admiral demanding to know why this particular cabin had not been cleared for action. Before the embarrassed captain had time to answer, Underwood, who was perfectly dressed in starched shirt, best uniform trousers and stable belt, turned from his task and announced to everyone in general and the admiral in particular that he was 'Very sorry about the inconvenience, but I thought everybody knew that Royal Marines officers always have clean sheets on Monday'!

*

I was once taught a salutary lesson about the morals of my brother officers. My ship, HMS Anzio, was playing the frigate HMS Zulu at rugger on HMS Jufair's sand pitch in Bahrain when I broke my leg. This was not really a tragedy but the unexpected result of this accident most certainly was. That night I had arranged to share a newly arrived Fortnum's hamper for two with a most attractive young girl who worked for the political resident. There were not many girls in Bahrain and so I considered the assignation a distinct coup over my rivals. Part of the meal needed to be cooked well in advance of the agreed hour for the tryst, and so she planned to start at about the time our rugger match was due to end.

Whilst lying on the touchline waiting for the ambulance I realized that it was vital to get a message through to the residency immediately to postpone our evening. The opposing team captain was a great friend of mine, also a Royal Marine, and so I explained very carefully what he had to do. He understood my predicament fully; too fully as it turned out.

Once in hospital I never saw my friend again in Bahrain as his ship sailed a few days later, and so it was nearly three weeks before I pieced together the history of my Christmas hamper. My friend had deliberately waited until he knew it was too late, before reporting at the girl's front door dressed in a dinner jacket. He had never met her before and as he was delivering my belated message he sniffed the air and asked, very politely, if he could by any chance smell pheasant and, possibly, Christmas pudding. The answer was, of course, 'Yes, and I'm sure that Ewen would not want it to be wasted!' Now I know never to trust even the closest of friends when sex and Fortnum's are irresistibly combined.

Admiral Sir Lindsay Bryson

A young sublieutenant in the Fleet Air Arm visited Sydney aboard a light fleet carrier just after the end of the Second World War. The first night in port he went ashore and had a whale of a time, as far as he could remember! What he did remember was inviting a large number of Sydney characters on board next night to the ship's cocktail party. He also remembered that this was a private cocktail party given by the admiral to entertain the Sydney elite.

Filled with apprehension he waited at the top of the gangway hoping that his drinking companions of the previous evening would recognize him – he was not at all sure that he would recognize them! They all seemed to recognize him and he whisked them away to a quiet corner before they could cause any trouble or embarrassment. He worked very hard to entertain them and appeared to have avoided any problems with his senior officers or the Sydney elite.

When 'beat the retreat' was over and all had gone he breathed a sigh of relief, but his sense of wellbeing evaporated when he was sent for by the admiral.

'Jolly good party tonight,' said the admiral. 'Lots of interesting guests! All the officers supported me well in helping to entertain them, but you, "Bloggs", were quite outstanding as a host, and I would like to thank you for all your efforts,' said the admiral with a twinkle in his eye.

'Bloggs' was never quite sure whether he had been rumbled or not!

Admiral of the Fleet
Sir Henry Leach

VE Day saw our destroyer working up in the practice areas of Alexandria having recently completed a refit. At about 1100 the petty officer telegraphist, grinning all over his face, came to the bridge brandishing a signal which had just been received in the wireless office. Since it was unclassified there was no reason why it should not be shown to anyone who happened to be around, and he did so. The signal was in fact an admiralty general message. It read quite simply: 'The war in Europe is over.'

Several officers and ratings were on the bridge at the time, including myself. We were, of course, delighted and displayed our feelings with some spirit. All of which attracted the attention of the commanding officer, seated in his chair. The CO was a lieutenant commander – clever, but disinclined to trust subordinates and with little understanding of, or regard for, sailors. He was shown the signal with some enthusiasm. It did not take long to read and evidently he did so several times. Then, with a deadpan face, he turned to the PO Tel. and asked: 'Is this genuine?' The cold hand of pedantic authority quickly dampened our exuberance. 'Oh God,' most of us thought, 'have we really got to have a great witch-hunt to check that the war is over when the admiralty has already told us that it is?' 'We will carry on with the exercises,' said the captain curtly. Here was a turn up for the book. The signal officer was summoned: a young Australian sublieutenant RNVR who didn't give a damn for anyone. Instructed to verify the signal, he did so. 'You could ask FOLEM, sir' (Flag Officer Levant and Eastern Mediterranean, the local senior naval officer at Alexandria), one of us suggested.

But the CO saw through this one. Ever with an eye to the main chance he realized that if the AGM was valid, in challenging it he would appear an ass. Equally, if it was a hoax, it would reflect ill on the ship (and him) to bring it to the notice of his admiral. A catch-22 situation and the captain discarded the option.

By this time the news had spread all round the ship. Most of the rest of the officers had come to the bridge, amongst them the first lieutenant. A big, imperturbable, sensible man, liked and respected by all, he quickly grasped the situation. 'I don't think, sir,' he quietly put to the CO, 'that anyone's heart is really going to be in the exercises now or that any real value is likely to be derived from them. If you are still not prepared to accept the signal why don't you turn back towards Alex and see if any other ship appears to have got the message?'

After some further argument the captain reluctantly agreed to this proposition. Course was reversed and we headed back down the Great Pass towards Alexandria. As we neared the harbour we were met by the cacophony of many sirens being sounded incessantly, and when closer still we could see that every ship had dressed overall with flags.

An ass? Let us just say that the captain was the only man in the squad in step.

*

The 14th Destroyer Flotilla in the eastern Mediterranean contained a variety of characters. Two in particular were notorious for their voracious appetites and their remarkable capacity at table. They were the gannets of the flotilla and known as such. One was a lieutenant RN; the other a sublieutenant RNVR who subsequently became a senior civil servant.

As part of the VJ celebrations an eating competition between the two gannets was arranged. It took place in the Union Bar in Alexandria, a favourite haunt for wardrooms taking a run ashore. The rules were simple: 'go' time, 1900; drinks and small eats provided by the supporters to taste for thirty minutes; contestants to their table at 1930; then eat and drink. The winner to be the one who consumed the greatest number of courses, each accompanied by an appropriate beverage. No time limit, but undue delay (other than short-term visits of necessity) to result in disqualification. There was just one bizarre aspect: the sequence of courses was to be in reverse.

Thus the menu started with coffee and crème de menthe, proceeded backwards through fruit and port, rum baba and sauterne, T-bone steak and claret, curried prawns, rice and beer, to consommé and sherry. A surviving contestant (and both were tipped to be in this category) was to return to additional helpings of curried prawns, rice and beer until, one way or another, he indicated that the limit of his capacity had been reached.

On the night of the competition there was a festive air about the Union Bar. The contestants' wardrooms were well represented and there was no shortage of umpires – themselves indulging in a more normal, less gourmand repast. A good deal of money changed hands.

As predicted by the form guards, both contestants completed the prescribed menu albeit with some diminution of vigour and incisiveness of speech. After a brief adjournment (by mutual consent), they re-entered their table for the munch up to the finish.

The RN lieutenant succumbed when he was half way through his second helping of curried prawns and rice. But the

RNVR sub., a man of bigger (or more elastic) stomach, was bent on a really convincing victory and threw in his napkin only when well advanced into his third helping.

The Sudanese waiters were riveted.

Military Mania

Sir Paul Hawkins
Member of Parliament

A German general on inspection of a POW camp found British officers feeding a German guard dog and was furious.

Next day on parade the German interpreter read out an order as follows: 'Here is an order from the OKW (German High Command) for all British POWs: German guard dogs as from today have been strictly forbidden to accept food from British POWs. British POWs, please note.'

Dr Robert Runcie
The Archbishop of Canterbury

On the day the war ended I was instructed to receive the surrender of a small town in Schleswig-Holstein. As a young subaltern I was very conscious of my position and of the solemnity and formality of the occasion. I felt it would be enhanced by the setting – at the top of the steps of the town hall. I was determined to make the most of it. At that moment I was *Great Britain*.

My car drew up. Guns were at the ready to defend me. I ascended the steps. All around me were the faces of curious children and rather cowed civilians.

The German commander emerged, supported by his aides. Clearly he had prepared for his moment of humiliation by a lunch at which the wine flowed freely.

With a broad smile he flung his arms around me and greeted me: 'Welcome, Herr Lieutenant, come and have a drink.'

I was completely non-plussed. My pomposity was punctured. There was only one answer. Into the town hall I went and we all drank each other's health. It was totally against the rules and I haven't dared tell the story for forty years.

Michael Mates
Member of Parliament

Dress rehearsal for the Sovereign's Parade on a snow-covered square at Sandhurst. The band is playing, and the adjutant on his charger is inspecting the cadets. A snowball projected from somewhere in the ranks strikes the charger on the quarters. The adjutant, unmoved, shouts, 'Take his name, sergeant major.'

'Got 'im, sir,' replies the RSM on the instant.

'Take his name, drill sergeant.'

'Got 'im, sir,' shouts the drill sergeant without hesitation.

'Take that gentleman cadet to the guardroom.'

'Got 'im, sir,' reply two NCOs in unison, and a cadet is doubled away, feet barely touching the ground.

When the adjutant came to inspect the band his steely eye noticed that the bass drummer only had one drumstick. Upon enquiring why, the drummer answered, 'The woollen head of the drumstick flew off some minutes ago as I was twirling it. I'm afraid I did not see where it went.'

Brigadier J. W. F. Rucker

Throughout my army career, I have always been involved in cricket, playing or organizing or scoring or just watching in blissful idleness. Without doubt, the most competitive and demanding experiences of my life centred in my eldest son Rupert's boys' family cricket matches. As the summer hols approached each year our collective energies were dedicated to fiendishly tricky decisions of selecting the opponent, then the team, laying on the teas, umpires, scorers, pitch, groundsman, special rules, numbers of overs – it was all needle stuff and the agony if you got it wrong, the ghastly recriminations in defeat and the oh so sweet triumph in victory!

One famous match lives on to remind us all how narrow is the gap between triumph and disaster. Of course, I should have known better; the match was on the RAC Centre Pitch at Bovington, the opponents under the steely leadership of a colonel in the Royal Tank Regiment, anxious as ever to take the Cavalry to the cleaners (we're all great friends, really). The Ruckers win the toss and elect to field, the sun shines, the ball swings merrily in the breeze and wickets fall briskly as Rupert, Jeremy and Jonathan, bowling like boys inspired, pile on the pressure. Soon the enemy are 10 for 9, a row of long faces in the pavilion. Out strides the Colonel of Tanks – his last man is missing, but there's this boy who is somebody's cousin, just gone to Milton Abbey (a bit off as all the other boys are still at prep school), would I mind, in the circumstances? – I mean it's unlikely to make much difference now. Yes, of course he can come in! Rupert and Co. doubtful but trying to be sporting about it all. Well, in strides this chap, not very big but looks useful and confident. He takes two fours off Rupert's next over then, while the other batsman still left in blocks stolidly, he sets about the bowling with rare skill and relish. He passes his 50 seven overs later, and goes on to an undefeated 79 taking his team's total to 110!

No one spoke to me at tea. I tried the cheerful, positive, there's a run bonanza out there approach, but it was no good. As I feared, that wretched boy opened the bowling and just the way he polished the ball on the back of his trousers portended disaster. Our brave opening pair lasted two overs but then the floodgates burst and our sorrow was nothing on Sodom and Gomorrah as an endless stream of woebegone figures trailed out to the wicket and back to the pavilion. We were all out for 21 – their mysterious hero having taken 8 for 6.

Somehow we put a brave face on it. The Royal Tank Regiment thought we had been jolly sporting which we bore smilingly with murder in our hearts. 'Well Dad,' said Rupert, 'I hope you've learnt your lesson. Don't you ever let anyone off the hook like that again.' I could only manage a humble nod of acknowledgement.

Major E. L. T. Capel

When the war began I was in Wales, serving as an instructor at a militia training depot. Close on eleven o'clock we assembled in the marquee, which did duty as the officers' mess, to hear what Mr Chamberlain had to say. When he finished speaking there was an immense feeling of relief that, at long last, the waiting was over. Champagne corks popped . . .

When the war ended I was in Italy. On 29 April 1945 the German forces there surrendered. I felt no elation, only a feeling of total anticlimax. I just wanted to go to sleep. . .

A very short time later I was posted to a staff job in Egypt. The senior staff officer who interviewed me when I reported for duty was extremely formal, and he rapidly put the Second World War in perspective by stating ' . . . now that that unpleasant little incident is over, we regulars must make it our business to get the army back to prewar standards. It's up to us. The really important task starts now.'

I began to wonder what the hell I had been doing for the last six years. . .

Brigadier M. J. Wilkes

A very pretty WRAC assistant adjutant had been put on the top table to divert a number of very senior officers. After a good deal of small talk the conversation turned to military matters and the poor girl became increasingly bored. Sensing this, one senior gentleman desperately tried to involve her in the conversation by asking abruptly whether, given the circumstances, she would be able to kill a man. A silence fell upon the company. By this time furious, she simply lowered her eyelashes, ran her tongue over her lips and breathed that, given the circumstances, she thought that she certainly could and that it would take her about two weeks to accomplish it!

Lord Carrington
Secretary General, NATO

At the beginning of 1945, when I was commanding a squadron of tanks in Germany, my squadron and the infantry company with which we worked fought a small battle. This was not an unqualified success, and the brigadier took the view that the company commander of the infantry battalion and I had read the map wrong, gone the wrong way and generally made a complete nonsense of our task. There was a *very* small element of truth in this. We stood to attention in front of him while, purple with indignation, and even more articulate than usual, he revealed his innermost thoughts about us. This lasted some time. As I listened I saw approach behind him a large and very angry billygoat. In view of the circumstances, and not wishing to interrupt him, I did not think it necessary to warn the brigadier of the approach of this addition to the party. The billygoat, which was clearly as angry as the brigadier and probably with more reason, charged. With a murderous look the brigadier got painfully to his feet, removed his pistol from its holster and discharged its contents at the goat. The goat, satisfied that its assault had been successful, pottered away unharmed. The brigadier looked sharply at me, burst out laughing, got into his jeep and drove away.

Brigadier Helen Meechie
Director, Women's Royal Army Corps

The proposal that members of the WRAC might be armed for self-defence went through many years of deliberation. Even after the army had decided that there was merit in the proposal, the then Secretary of State directed that there should be more research into public opinion. Those closest involved, i.e. members of the WRAC, had definite opinions, whatever public opinion might offer. Witness one conversaton between the then DWRAC and a junior NCO serving in BAOR.

DWRAC: You know that the idea that WRAC should be armed for self-defence is under consideration.
JNCO: Yes, I had heard.
DWRAC: If it were your decision as to which weapon

you should have, what would be your answer?
JNCO: A Chieftain tank, preferably ready to move westwards!

Lord Mayhew

During the liberation of Belgium, we were told a multitude of resistance stories, and I was rather struck by this one.

A Belgian riding in a crowded train lit a cigarette with a match and threw the match out of the window. A German SS man asked him for a light. The Belgian hesitated, then handed his lighted cigarette over. The German lit his cigarette with it and handed it back. The Belgian then threw the cigarette out of the window.

General
Sir Martin Farndale
Commander-in-Chief, British Army of the Rhine

During the British army's exercise 'Lionheart' in September 1984, the biggest the British army had conducted since 1945, two amusing incidents occurred.

A company commander arrived in his battle area and was told to prepare a defensive position around a wooded hill which adjoined a large farm complex. He did his recce, gave his orders to his platoon commanders, and left his Company 2IC in charge while he went to battalion headquarters for orders. On his return he found the whole position quite different to that which he had ordered, and in a fury demanded of his 2IC 'What has been going on here? This is not what I told you to do!'

'Ah,' said the 2IC, 'after you had left, the German farmer who owns this land came out and saw what we were doing. He thought your plans could be improved, and, using his experience fighting the Russians in the Second World War, he suggested a much better way of defending this piece of ground. I am afraid that I thought he was right, and we have laid out the company accordingly!'

*

A battery commander arrived at a German village and wanted to dig in his field guns. This meant digging a series of very large holes. He wanted one of these to be near a German house. He therefore went to the house and asked if he could do it. The owner said that it would be quite all right and he saw no problems, but he suggested, 'Before you do, I think I should tell you that I am a regular soldier and I am a battery commander in the Orange Forces which are opposing you. If you do dig in here I shall take steps to ensure that you are knocked out when I join the exercise.'

Major J. C. Lillies
Head of Publicity, The Royal British Legion

In Germany in the mid-sixties it fell to my regiment to provide the guard for the local American nuclear munitions depot. Although rumour had it that the depot contained no nuclear warheads, the guard, which consisted of a full infantry platoon, had always to be on full alert and were often tested with practice alarms.

Although the orders were that everyone had to remain fully dressed at all times, the platoon commander was in the habit of removing his boots while he slept. His NCOs ensured that everyone else obeyed orders. With very little to occupy them on a guard which lasted several days, the men hit on a plan of revenge. While their commander slept, they filled his boots with raspberry jam from the 'compo' rations. The result exceeded their expectations as the authorities unwittingly called a practice turnout. The young officer rapidly hauled on his boots with a satisfying squelch and then had to rush around in the glutinous mess as though nothing was amiss!

From then on, to the platoon commander's fury, one of those mystery voices that sometimes plague radio nets, would often follow transmissions from that platoon headquarters callsign with the cry 'Jam Booty!'

Field-Marshal
Sir Edwin Bramall
Chief of the Defence Staff

I joined the army in August 1942 as a new recruit at a Primary Training Centre in York. Soon after we had assembled as a recruit platoon, the platoon sergeant, a veteran Cockney, decided it would be a good thing if we took some exercise and had a cricket match against a rival platoon or company. Having been captain of my school cricket XI, I think the other members of my platoon were expecting me to cut a bit of a dash, but then they were hardly allowing for our sergeant's perception of the noble game! For when we had all turned out on to what passed as a cricket field, in a wide variety of dress, the platoon sergeant said, 'Right, whose name begins with "A"?' (To which there were no takers.) 'Well then, whose name begins with "B"?'

So I said: 'Mine does, sergeant.'

'Right,' he said. 'You bat number eleven.'

At that moment one of the other members of my platoon piped up and said: 'Please, sergeant, Bramall is rather a good cricketer.'

To which the sergeant replied, 'I don't care if he is Donald Bradman himself, his name begins with "B" and he is batting number eleven.'

I believe it taught me from a very early stage the arbitrary nature of some military decisions and orders, and that if you were always looking for common sense and logic in the big bad world, you could have a rude shock coming!

*

On D Day itself I was heading for the beaches in an American tank landing craft. The night before we landed was extremely rough and, as orderly officer, it was all I could manage to get below decks to inspect the meals of my riflemen. And when I returned a bit worse for wear to the wardroom before turning in, which most of my brother officers had already wisely done, I was faced with a rather odd sight. For there was my very English, aristocratic commanding officer sitting by himself trying to read a book, while a black American sailor, who had come in to tidy up, was 'jitterbugging' round the room to the strains of a juke box turned full on, and getting himself entwined with the colonel's lanky legs! It struck me as most incongruous, although I may say the colonel seemed completely oblivious to the whole thing.

The next morning, when we were preparing to land, we had been given the strictest instruction to make out a next of kin card which, on landing over the beach, would be handed to the beachmaster for despatch home to records. This would tell everybody, including our families, that we had not been lost at sea and had arrived safely in France. These forms were then collected up in bundles and made the responsibility of the company second-in-command. As his turn came to drive off the landing ship, in his International half-track, he was clutching these things on the horizontal metal grille which, in battle, could be lowered to cover the windscreen. Unfortunately, the place which the ship had chosen to run aground had in front of it, and unbeknownst to anybody, a very deep pool, so that when the half-track drove forward off the unloading ramp it went straight into about eight feet of water. The result was that those valuable bundles of forms flew off the top of the vehicle and disappeared into the pounding surf where they were quickly washed away; and that was the last we heard or saw of them. Bureaucracy had been thwarted, but it did not appear to make the slightest difference one way or the other, and we went on to do the business that had to be done in the very heavy fighting around Caen.

The Right Honourable Lord Luke
Vice-president, The Royal British Legion

I was a TA officer for twelve years before the 1939 war, when of course I became mobilized and involved. All very serious but with lighter moments. An entirely new life began – what we had been waiting for or at least preparing for. It was something that we had a period of comparative calm in which to complete the change from civilian to military life, and through the first winter of the war it was possible to get some delicacies for the officers' mess before rationing began. The first winter of the war was a period of getting hardened and accustomed to army huts with boots frozen to the floor in the morning. Army jogging for officers and men (no exceptions) sorted out those leg muscles in no time!

The real activity began when I was ordered to form a new battalion from raw recruits, at the very time of the return from Dunkirk, without weapons – until Canadian rifles arrived – and, I seem to remember, 303 ammo did not fit. We had some difficulties in training and I had some difficulties forming a staff from the officers and others sent to me from the depot – they never sent their best.

However, within three months the GOC came down and asked if I was ready to take my unit up to defend the Norfolk coast against invasion. Of course I answered 'Yes', though I felt rather differently. So up we went and waited for enemy barges, having fortified the coast with pill boxes on the cliffs, scaffolding on the beaches and the sappers laid mines (which I am afraid are still troublesome). Every time a general came round he wanted the pill boxes somewhere else – and who was I among Generals? They were professionals – I was an amateur. Incidentally, pill boxes were constructed pretty solidly – not made for moving – and many are still *in situ*.

We withstood the rigours of the east coast. I still have the secret telegram which announced (in September 1940) that the moon and tide were just right for invasion. We 'stood to' for nights and days but no one came – so we settled down to serious training and drafting for the next few years.

Major-General P. I. Chiswell

Some years ago in the Near East, amidst the heat of a very hot day, a keen-eyed, sharp brigadier was inspecting a detached battalion of his brigade.

As he approached the immaculate huts which housed a rifle

company, the company sergeant major concerned suddenly spotted a very scruffy soldier hovering in the doorway of the hut nearest to the inspection party.

'Quick lad,' he whispered. 'Brigadier's coming, don't want him to see you in that state – hop in that cupboard.'

The brigadier entered the hut, he passed complimentary comments upon its cleanliness and, turning to the unsuspecting company commander, he asked, 'Have your soldiers enough cupboard space?'

'Yes, sir,' replied the company commander confidently.

'Well, let's see,' said the brigadier somewhat disbelievingly. 'Open that nearest cupboard.'

With embarrassment the sergeant major complied.

'What on earth are you doing in there?' barked the astonished brigadier.

'I am on leave, sir,' replied the solider.

Major-General
R. E. J. Gerrard Wright

Finishing line in a speech often used by me as a dinner guest: 'As you know, I am here to solve your problems. If you have one and we should happen to meet later during the evening – you're walking down the passage one way and I'm walking up it the other – please, just keep on walking!'

Field-Marshal Lord Carver

On 13 June 1944, 22nd Armoured Brigade, leading 7th Armoured Division, ran into trouble in and beyond Villers-Bocage, when the recently arrived 2nd Panzer Division counterattacked and cut the road between the villages of Amaye and Briquessard behind them. I was commanding 1st Royal Tank Regiment in support of 131st Lorried Infantry Brigade, which was following them up. The brigade commander, with one of its battalions, was up with 22nd Brigade, and was cut off with them. Bobbie Erskine, the divisional commander, ordered me to assume command of the rest of the brigade and to open up the road and join hands with 22nd Brigade next day.

Leaving 1/6th Queen's to secure Briquessard, I advanced with the regiment and one of the Queen's companies at first light, and soon cleared the road to Amaye, where we made contact with the 8th Hussars. Almost as soon as we had done so, our right flank was attacked by the panzers. We fought them off several times, knocking out several of their tanks, including at least one Tiger. In mid-afternoon they renewed their attack, and while the battle was raging, with armour-piercing shot whistling through the apple trees, I got a message on the wireless to say that the commander of 22nd Armoured Brigade, that splendid, gallant and eccentric cavalryman, 'Looney' Hinde, was coming to see me with fresh orders. When he arrived, I got out of my tank, reluctantly handing over command of the battle to my second-in-command, and walked the hundred yards to Looney's scout car. He started to tell me that General Erskine had ordered him to withdraw his whole brigade back to Briquessard during the night, and I was to act as rearguard and hold on to Amaye until everybody else was through, getting my own regiment back to the new line by first light. He had not finished his orders, when he suddenly said: 'Anybody got a matchbox?'

'What do you want one for?' I said.

56

'Do you see that caterpillar?' he replied. 'It's a very rare one. I must have it.'

'For God's sake, brigadier,' I protested, 'I've got a tense battle on my hands. We can't waste time on caterpillars.'

'Don't be such a bloody fool, Mike,' was his answer. 'You have a battle every day of your life: you don't see a caterpillar like that once in fifteen years!'

The Right Honourable Nicholas Winterton
Member of Parliament

I am reminded of the occasion when four men were travelling by train northwards to London. After a while, one of the number said, 'Well, gentlemen, as we appear to be in for a long journey together, shall we introduce ourselves? I am a brigadier in the army, and I have one son who has recently been commissioned in the army.'

The next man said, 'That's strange, I am also a brigadier in the army, and I have one son who is a lieutenant in the army.'

Then the third one said, 'How extraordinary! I am also a brigadier, and I have one son who has just been promoted to captain in the army.'

Then they all looked at the fourth man who said, 'Well, gentlemen, I am also in the army, but only a sergeant major. However, I have three sons in the army, and they're all brigadiers.'

Colonel J. Hughes
Former Chairman of the Poppy Appeal

When the Americans first arrived in the UK early in 1942, as a young gunnery instructor I had the task of introducing some of their officers to the BOFORS AA gun. In the course of my lecture to a squad of some twenty officers I said that the BOFORS was a 'dual-purpose weapon', in that while its main function was to engage low-flying aircraft with a percussion shell, it could also be used against tanks using an armour-piercing solid shot. Whereupon a colonel from the deep south drawled, 'Captain, ah reckon there was only one dual-purpose weapon ever made and the good God gave that to man!'

*

The very amorous brigadier had a rather nubile ATS driver. After some months, during which their relationship progressed, the young driver came to the brigadier's office and said, 'Sir, I have good news and bad news for you. Which would you prefer first?'

'It's Monday morning – let's have the good news first.'

'Well, sir,' she replied, 'the good news is that you're *not* sterile after all!'

*

Instructor at the Joint-Services Staff College, finishing his evening lecture and looking at his watch, said: 'Well, gentlemen, it is now ten p.m. I beg your pardon – for the army officers present, it is 2200 hours; for the navy, it is four bells;

58

and for the RAF, the big hand is at twelve and the small one at ten.'

*

At the annual conference or 'congregation' of military chaplains, a rabbi and a Roman Catholic priest found themselves exchanging views. 'Tell me,' said the rabbi, 'why do you wear your collar back to front?'

'Because I'm a father,' replied the priest.

'But I'm also a father,' said the rabbi, 'and I don't wear my collar back to front.'

'Yes, but I'm the father of thousands,' answered the priest.

After a lengthy pause for thought the rabbi countered, 'Well, perhaps in that case you should have worn your trousers back to front as well.'

*

A rather rebellious private, often in trouble, went to the sergeant major who was always giving him stick and asked, 'May I have weekend leave, sir?'

'Certainly not,' said the RSM, 'You've already had all the leave you're entitled to.'

'Well it's like this, sir,' pleaded the private, 'My wife serves in WRAC and I've just had a letter from her telling me that she has just been promoted to sergeant major.'

'So what?' thundered the RSM.

'Well, sir,' replied the private, 'I'd like to go home to fulfil a lifelong ambition.'

*

A very tough RSM was having trouble with a rather dim Private Smith who was invariably late on parade. 'What you should do,

Smith,' said the sergeant major, in that kindly tone of voice they have, 'is to get up at 6 a.m. and hang your bare backside out of your barrack room window.'

'Why should I do that, sir?' naively inquired Private Smith.

'To give your brains an airing before breakfast,' said the RSM.

Next morning, to the RSM's great surprise, there was Private Smith first man on parade. 'What's this, Smith, were you up all night?'

'No sergeant major, I did as you told me,' he replied, 'I hung my bare backside out of the window this morning.'

'You what?' thundered the RSM, appalled at the results of his sarcasm. 'I hope no one saw you?'

'Oh yes, sir, the colonel walked past,' was the reply.

'The colonel?' exploded the sergeant major. 'And what did he say?'

'He only said, "Good morning, sergeant major." '

Sir David Scott
Chairman, Ellerman Lines

During 1942 the anti-aircraft brigade headquarters at Harrow-on-the-Hill, of which I was a member, was disbanded as part of a general reorganization of the air defences of the United Kingdom. As a consequence of this decision the assets of the officers' mess had to be liquidated in fairly short order. (Those of the assets which were already liquid were separately disposed of, but that is another story on which my memory is unaccountably blurred!)

The most immediate problem was the disposal of the small flock of hens which for some months past had uncomplainingly converted the mess swill into breakfast eggs. After discussion it was unanimously agreed that the hens should be divided amongst the members of the mess, each officer being allowed to choose and despatch one bird.

It was a dull afternoon, with a hint of drizzle in the air. One by one my colleagues let themselves into the chicken run (the brigadier alone had been given dispensation to delegate the task to his batman), and with greater or less expertise had wrung the neck of the chicken of their choice. When it came to my turn, however, I was deeply humiliated to find myself incapable of executing the task. Even recalling Churchill's sombre warning to Hitler – 'Some chicken, some neck' – did little to restore my bruised self-confidence. After about four ineffective attempts, which left me in a progressively worse condition than the intended victim and up to the ankles in damp manure, I came to the conclusion that only one honourable course was open to me. Holding the chicken's slippery and by then somewhat part-worn neck firmly in my left hand, I took my service revolver resolutely from its holster, pressed the muzzle firmly to the point of its jaw, and pulled the trigger.

There was an enormous report, seemingly far louder than that of the 3.7 inch anti-aircraft guns to which by that time I was relatively accustomed. When the smoke cleared away, the job was undoubtedly done. Later in the day I presented to my wife a headless, but nonetheless welcome, addition to her rations. It happily turned out that this was the only occasion during the entire war when I was called upon to put my revolver to lethal use.

The Right Honourable
Francis Pym
Member of Parliament

The regiment had a long approach march to the Gothic Line in northern Italy where an attack was planned for the beginning of September 1944. In the lead was a despatch rider, Lance Corporal Philson. In the course of this move an irate officer of another formation stopped Philson and slanged him for five minutes, without taking breath, for leading the regiment up the wrong route. This was, in fact, an entirely false accusation. Philson stood quietly until he could get a word in, and then replied: 'Beg pardon, sir, but in spite of the fact that I am a lance corporal I was not consulted before the regiment was sent up this route!' No officer could have been rebuked more tactfully.

Sir Timothy Bevan
Chairman, Barclays Bank

I was seventeen when I joined the Scots Guards in early 1945 and so was at Pirbright as a guardsman when VJ Day dawned. I was not really military material and rapidly discovered that the middle rank was the one to be in; if you were in the first you had to be keen and if you were in the third you were obviously malingering. I have, thankfully, forgotten my number, which one had frequently to repeat to those in authority, though they knew perfectly well who we were. For years it haunted me like a number from Alcatraz.

We were in a brigade squad commanded by various insensitive brigade sergeants who frequently and loudly despaired of ever being able to make anything of us, though I felt they were unnecessarily pessimistic. We also presumed, with the optimism of youth, that a heart of gold beat beneath the ferocity, but that theory was never proved.

VJ Day at camp was much like any other, except that we were expressly forbidden to go to London in the evening. So, naturally, after the last parade, a group of us made our way, without the necessary passes, to London, but being reasonably 'fly' (or observant), we disembarked at Clapham Junction – which we knew did not boast military policemen, unlike which Waterloo certainly did.

Then, like the rest of London, we cheered outside Buckingham Palace, drank and, I presume, ate – and missed the last train back to Woking. So we decided to catch the milk train back in the morning, and for the night – well, my parents' house in Chelsea was empty, my father being on his demob leave in the West Country. My mother, who was kindly but firm, had always said I could have friends to stay when they were away, provided – and it was a point she stressed with some force that her bedroom was not used.

However, since there were not enough beds to go round, we stripped the bedding off my parents' bed, put the mattress on the floor and two guardsmen slept on the mattress and two more in the bed – I think they took their boots off – and the rest slept on the floor.

Come the dawn, we caught, again at Clapham Junction, the early train to Woking and marched back to camp.

All was well – the sergeant who had told us not to go to London was in the same train back, but for form's sake we did not see each other.

But the real crisis was at hand – my parents' disturbed bed. It took several telephone calls and £10 (£110 in today's money) to Mrs Richardson, the 'daily' in Chelsea, to get her to iron the sheets and redo the bed, so that all evidence of unwashed, and not totally sober, guardsmen was eradicated.

It was not till the 1970s that I at last owned up.

And what has become of the party of celebratory guardsmen? One is a peer of the realm, one was chairman of a brewery, one is the governor of the Bank of England – the very epitome of propriety – and the rest I have forgotten. I suppose they have developed middle-aged spread and a veneer of respectability.

Sir Jeremy Morse
Chairman, Lloyds Bank

While serving as a second lieutenant in Rafah in 1948, I was asked to sit on a field court martial, there being a shortage of more senior officers. The first defendant was a private in the Ordnance Corps who was charged with stealing stores. After the evidence I was horrified to be asked to give my verdict first: it was explained to me that this was the rule, designed to prevent my being swayed by my two senior colleagues. I thought that the defendant was probably guilty but the prosecution had not really *proved* it; so, remembering from school that 'a man is innocent until proven guilty', I said, 'Not guilty.' The other two promptly said, 'Guilty,' which became the majority verdict. I was then even more horrified to be asked to give my sentence first. Feeling that I had been rather lenient in suggesting that he was not guilty, I decided not to underdo it and said, 'Two years' detention.' The other two each said, 'One week,' and the chairman then added up and divided by three. So justice was done, and I was proved innocent.

General Sir Patrick Howard-Dobson
National President, The Royal British Legion

A Falklands fable:

PARA (*tired of yomping and hoping for a lift*): 'How fast does your Scorpion go, mate?'
HOUSEHOLD CAVALRYMAN (*homesick*): 'Oh, 'bout as fast as the Quorn on a good scenting day.'

Rear-Admiral J. J. Black

Two retired army officers were sitting together in the 'RAG' discussing the shortcomings of the modern generation.

'Do you know,' said the general, 'I was telling my daughter-in-law that my great-grandfather was killed at Waterloo. She looked up with a sympathetic expression and said, 'Oh, how sad; on which platform did it happen?'

'Ridiculous,' said the brigadier, 'as if it mattered which platform it was on!'

Lieutenant-Colonel T. R. Forrest
Secretary, The Union Jack Club

At the guards' depot, the company offices of the five foot guards regiments were situated in one straight line, side by side, with no distinguishing mark to suggest which was which, apart from the appropriate regimental sign on the company office door.

One enterprising company sergeant major decided that his

company would erect a flagpole and fly the regimental flag and did so, only to be followed in short order by the other four companies.

Unknown to the others, one of this merry band of gentlemen decided that *his* company should have a flagpole taller than any of the others, so one dark night a suitable 'fighting patrol' was organized and the light of the new day showed that all of the other flagpoles had been suitably sawn to reduce them in height to a height less than his.

The culprit was obvious! What followed is best left to the imagination!

*

The commanding officer decreed that a battalion 'garden competition' should be held, to be judged at a suitable date in September by his wife – a keen and knowledgeable gardener.

Each company was allowed a sum of money from PRI Funds with which to buy seeds, etc., and plenty of notice was given.

All of the companies – except one – planned their allocated gardens most meticulously, bought seeds and plants and filled the ground. The odd one out did nothing, and the day of judgement duly arrived.

It so happened that the 'odd one out' was the last to be judged, and by the time the commanding officer's wife reached the suspect company lines a transformation had taken place. The garden was immaculate, and full of daffodils!

The judge's gardening expertise soon caused her to realize that daffodils in *September* were a little out of season and on investigating more closely she soon discovered the flowers to be made of plastic!

It transpired that at about that time the NAAFI were giving away plastic daffodils with each packet of washing powder purchased, and someone in authority in the company had caused each man in the company to purchase the same but to donate his free flower to the company garden.

Lieutenant-Colonel D. H. Boydell
Member of National Executive Council,
The Royal British Legion

For much of the 1939–45 war I commanded first an army troops company and then a field company, both of the Indian Sappers and Miners.

In the autumn of 1943 we occupied what had been a French barracks in the Lebanon, and there we undertook to train the pioneer platoons of the three battalions of a Gurkha brigade in their trades and in field engineering. One morning, on visiting the workshops, I found a Gurkha squatting outside with blood pouring from his head and one of my sappers mopping it up with a piece of cotton waste. I asked what had happened and the sapper replied, 'Well, sahib, I was teaching him to use a chisel and he scratched his head with it.'

*

One of my subalterns was teaching the use of explosives. Having laid a number of charges, he said, 'Now we must take cover while the charges are fired.'

A Gurkha *havildar* (sergeant) said, 'Sahib, couldn't we stay here and watch what happens?'

*

The end of the war in Europe found us on the River Adige in northern Italy. The news of the German surrender was closely followed by orders to move to Taranto to build compounds for German prisoners who were surrendering in their thousands. VE Day found us in convoy travelling south.

We had almost completed the compounds on a former American bomber airfield when an American air force officer arrived with the news that several hundred bombs in dumps alongside the airfield were now unsafe and would have to be blown up *in situ*. Accordingly, about 50,000 German prisoners were marched some three miles into the country while the bombs were blown, and then marched back again. The camp commandant held a conference on the evening before to give his orders for this performance. Some of the German officers expressed concern lest the Indian sepoys who were to guard them might be a bit trigger-happy. The commandant replied, 'You will be all right so long as you keep strictly to the line of march, but I shouldn't advise anyone to stray.' As a result of this statement only three prisoners were missing at the end of the exercise, and they were soon recaptured.

It was then necessary to repair most of the Nissen huts in the compounds, which looked as if some enormous animal had sat on them. By early August all the work was completed and we were then ordered back to northern Italy to carry out various works between Venice, Trieste and the Austrian frontier.

VJ Day found us in convoy travelling north!

Units of 39 Infantry Brigade, Northern Ireland

The Devonshire Regiment drove down the road from Celle to Minden in late April 1958 to amalgamate with the Dorset Regiment. There were daily RSM's drill parades to prepare for the Amalgamation Parade on 17 May 1958. As was the normal form then, the RSM sent idle soldiers off parade at the double to the guardroom. He picked on a different company daily, locking up six or seven soldiers each time. C Coy, which was a Devon company, had seven men put away and after the drill parade the CSM sent the company orderly sergeant (who was a corporal) to the guardroom. Before he departed the CSM briefed him carefully saying, 'Give my compliments to Sergeant Gracie, the provost sergeant (who was a Dorset). Tell him you have come to collect the C Coy "Idle on Parade" and that they will be dealt with instantly and strongly.'

The company orderly sergeant went off to the guardroom, knocked on the door and said, 'Sergeant Gracie, compliments of . . . 'and got no further because the door opened and he was yanked inside to join the rest of the company in the cells. Eventually the CSM arrived, collected them all and doubled them away to the company office. On arrival he asked the company orderly sergeant what went wrong.

The COS replied, 'I only said "Sergeant Gracie, compliments of . . ." and was yanked inside.'

The CSM burst into laughter. 'Of course,' he said. 'You wouldn't know his surname is *Fields*, Gracie is his nickname.'

*

The battalion had a tented training camp at Pissouri jetty on the coast near Episkopi where reinforcements were acclimatized and given continuation training, and the battalion ran its cadres, MT, signals and so on. The camp CSM was a Second World War veteran MM BEM, and with the figure of a CSM in a Giles cartoon. He was also eccentric. The daily newspapers from England arrived in the camp in the very late evening, but the CSM would not allow them to be distributed to the messes and the soldiers NAAFI as 'papers were to be read at breakfast', so they were locked away till next morning. The sergeants' mess tent was a marquee and the mess had a proper wooden door. Every morning the CSM would enter and, with a great flourish, would shout, 'Good morning, gentlemen', glance around the mess and remove his peaked cap and pace stick which was always wedged under his arm, even when he wore swimming trunks. The few mess members each had their own newspaper, crisply folded on their side plate; the CSM's was the only *Daily Mirror*. One morning in particular the CSM entered the mess in his usual manner, glanced around and shouted, 'As you were, I'll do that again', and disappeared outside. He had spotted the MT sergeant reading his *Daily Mirror*. The sergeant quickly folded the newspaper and placed it on the CSM's plate, and waited for the thunder. The CSM re-entered in his usual way as if nothing had happened but added, 'I don't like a cross word at breakfast but take five extras, sergeant,' and promptly fell about the mess laughing at his own joke. He was laughing so much he could only manage a mug of tea for his breakfast.

*

Following a recent TV advertisement for the Japanese electrical firm called Toshiba, the handover between battalions in West Belfast became somewhat noisy. Soldiers in West Belfast wear a flak jacket called an 'Iniba jacket', and the security bases rang with cries of, 'Hello Jock, got an Iniba?' as members of the 3rd

Battalion the Royal Green Jackets greeted the incoming Jocks of the Gordon Highlanders.

*

Comments from the Northern Ireland nightly situation report

'Local Hood Hero nails himself to the wall'. Niall McCormish (name changed) redecorated the hall of his house when his homemade hand grenade with nails attached exploded. McCormish passed away 'piecefully!'

Brigade summary: A quiet day and wet evening.
Incidents: 2330 hours 3 UDR. Downpatrick RUC reported an explosion in the town hall. On investigating it was found the lavatory had collapsed making a loud bang, much dust and many red cheeks!

*

It is not only the British Army officer's upper lip which is stiff – apparently his thought processes are equally rigid!

*

Overheard on the RUC radio net:

There's a shattered window. There's no hole but it's badly shattered.

71

The garage is owned by a deceased member of the community.

To UB 40 from Uniform, check the alleyway at 796876 – suspicious movement reported.
   Acknowledged.
   To Uniform from UB40. We are at the alleyway. There's a lad here with a girl. His trousers are round his ankles, but he's now putting them back on and we are taking no further action!

★

Text of a signal following a suspected bomb explosion which had turned out to be the explosion when two men attempting to steal cable from underneath the Albert Bridge cut through the main electricity cable:

Following information may be of use: Two men now positively identified as Sean 'Sockets' Smith and Anthony 'Plugs' Quinn, well known on the circuit as the 'Sparky Boys'. Both considered to be down-to-earth live wires, flashy dressers with burning ambitions to make an impact on the area. Situation now seems to be defused although both men are somewhat browned off after their recent contact with the national grid. After their current experience it is unlikely that these two electrifying characters will generate any more negative waves for some time!

★

The Royal Scots Greys were exercising on the Soltau training area in Germany and it was a very quiet night. The regiment was awaiting an attack and the radios were silent. The quiet was broken by a call: 'Hello Zero . . . I am bloody bored.' Quick as a flash the regimental signals officer replied, 'Hello unknown station, this is Zero, say again Callsign.' There was a moment's hesitation until the unknown Scotsman retorted, 'Hello Zero, I'm not *that* bloody bored!'

*

A guardsman, on his final commanding officer's interview, asks to keep his rifle on discharge, as he had rescued it from Dunkirk, stood with it for hours outside Buckingham Palace, marched with it over long distances and cleaned and polished it continuously. The commanding officer grants the request and the guardsman is seen marching away from the barracks with his rifle at the shoulder.

Before retiring, the guardsman had prepared his house and garden – especially the latter. His wife was therefore totally amazed to see him digging up the lawn and laying down a mass of concrete. He then proceeded to mount his rifle on a plinth and, as he stood back to admire his handiwork, he was heard to exclaim, 'Now rust, you bastard!'

*

In the summer of 1984, an escape and evasion exercise was run in Sauerland area of West Germany. The exercise involved four-man 'bricks' travelling down a pre-planned escape route, living on minimal rations. They were instructed to supplement their diet by 'living off the land'.

On the second day of the exercise a brick was moving through a wood when they heard two Jocks arguing. 'Let's kill it,' said one, 'I'm starving . . . I'm on a seafood diet – see food and I eat it!' The other one was saying, 'Aw, you cannae kill it, it's so cuddly.'

Intrigued by this the first brick met up with the two Jocks whose voices they had heard. They found one clutching a beautiful, fluffy white rabbit with the other looking on with hungry eyes. As soon as the other brick appeared the Jock holding the rabbit jumped up and said, 'Look what we've got, we're going awa to eat it.' It materialized that the rabbit had come from a back garden and was a family pet belonging to a little girl.

Anyway, at the end of the exercise everyone had their own war story to tell. The brick who had found the rabbit were saying, 'Oh, we ate well, we had roast rabbit. It was fair good!' Of course everyone had to own up to what damage they had done. That brick owned up to eating a rabbit found at a house the location of which they gave.

The company commander who ran the exercise had to go round and give compensation to farmers who had turnips missing and the odd hen less.

He went to the house where the rabbit had come from. He found the owner and said to him, 'I believe you are missing a white rabbit.'

The owner said, 'No, not that I know of.'

The major said, 'But you must be.' The German said, 'No, come and have a look.' They went round to the back of the house, and there in the hutch was the white rabbit – alive and well – without any bits missing. The Jocks had put him back again! It just goes to show that even the toughest soldiers have big hearts.

*

A platoon's worth of officer cadets from Sandhurst were on their final exercise, before commissioning, in the Eiffel region of Germany.

One night, an eager, would-be platoon commander was tasked to move his complete platoon to a new patrol base some five kilometres away. Many will realize that achieving this aim without a major hitch is nigh on a physical impossibility for a group of officer cadets.

To offset the distinct probability of the whole force getting totally geographically embarrassed, the commander gave his orders to his sections in the minutest detail and picked the most obvious spot on his map as the final RV.

Three hours later the bold platoon commander was sitting alone in the RV. Sad as it is to relate, so were all the sections; they were all alone as well. The dreadful truth dawned on each and every one of them. Someone had blundered.

The gallant commander, being an embryonic leader of men, without hesitation, made his command decision to retrieve the dire situation which was threatening his Queen's commission. By means of his radio he asked his section commanders if they could see the moon. They all confirmed that they could. The platoon commander's reply was to the point. 'Well, head for it. I am right underneath it at the edge of the wood by the road.'

Within minutes the whole platoon was happily reunited. It was indeed a moonlit night.

Field-Marshal Sir Roland Gibbs

He was really a very good chap; perhaps a little pompous and hot-tempered, certainly a very good commander. But he happened to be asked to a regimental officers' mess dinner where the PMC was a well-known practical joker.

He left later than he had planned (for he had an early start next day), having dined extremely well, although not entirely convinced that he had made the impression he had wished.

'Goodnight, sir. Have a smooth journey home,' said the PMC as the staff car door was held open.

At the guardroom the barrier was down. The sentry approached the driver and apologetically reported that he had to search the car. 'Don't be ridiculous, sentry,' said the commander from the back seat. 'You know who I am, don't you, or you should. Let me get on. I am in a hurry.'

'Sorry, sir. Those are my orders,' said the sentry. 'Could you please open up the boot.'

'Send for the guard commander,' said the commander, exasperated and at the end of his tether.

'I am sorry,' said the guard commander, who had appeared on the scene, 'but the adjutant's orders are that no car is to leave the barracks without being searched.'

'Oh, very well,' said the commander, believing that it would be quicker to submit to a search than get an officer on the telephone. Out got the driver and opened up the boot of the car, and there, for the sentry, the guard commander and the commander (who had joined them) to see, was the whole of the officers' mess silver!

The Right Honourable
Lord Boyd-Carpenter

During the summer of 1940 I was serving as an ensign with the Training Battalion Scots Guards at Pirbright.

Towards mid-summer the civilian air-raid sirens sounded, and in accordance with the standing orders of London District we left our huts and proceeded to slit trenches close to the camp.

Nothing happened and we stood looking at the peaceful sky of a summer night. I found myself close to our regimental sergeant major; the famous and formidable Fred Archer. Like most junior officers I was nervous of this five foot six inch high dynamo and I remarked to him, by way of conversation, that the move to the slit trenches seemed to have gone very well.

'Yes, sir,' he said, 'very well indeed. But there is something the matter with the enemy, sir. They are idle.' (In Guards' regiments the word 'idle' is the ultimate in condemnation.)

Given that at that moment the Forces of the German Reich were overwhelming the last bits of resistance in Western Europe from the North Cape to the Mediterranean, this remark struck me as very entertaining and a peal of unsoldierly laughter echoed out over the silent trenches.

★

In August 1940 I was the junior officer of a detachment of my regiment which was doing local ground defence at RAF Fighter Command Headquarters at Stanmore. The Battle of Britain was being fought from Stanmore and in recognition of this the King and Queen (now Her Majesty the Queen Mother) came to visit the operations room underground and to lunch with the RAF.

As the junior officer of our detachment, I was left on duty while my detachment commander was lunching in the RAF mess with the royals.

Just as their majesties had emerged from the operations room and were, I was told, enjoying a pre-lunch glass of sherry, my telephone rang and the local sub-district headquarters (who were our immediate superiors) informed me that there was a report of parachutists landing about half a mile from the Fighter Command Headquarters.

In the atmosphere of that time it seemed only too like the efficiency of the Germans that they would put down parachutists and take Fighter Command and the King and Queen all

77

in one. So I saw myself, for some ugly minutes, as being the man who lost the war!

Obviously one closed up the wire, issued ammunition and called in reinforcements. Their Majesties, to their surprise, were persuaded to go back to the operations room which they thought they had finished inspecting.

I was not even able to get my detachment commander on the telephone since an awestruck WAAF said I could not speak to him as he was speaking to the King!

It turned out, however, that the report which the sub-district had taken so literally had come from the Royal Observer Corps who had sighted some picnickers' paper bags blowing about in the wind on a north London common.

Captain E. G. Williams
Member of the National Executive Council,
The Royal British Legion

Although discipline was strict, as in any military hospital, it was not difficult for an ambulatory patient to escape detection for long enough to enjoy a 'chota-peg' or two at the Planters' Club. Certainly I can recall no real feeling of guilt on that particular afternoon in January 1943, when my wandering footsteps carried me in that direction.

On my arrival at the club the first person I met was a bearded sailor who, in sudden recognition, greeted me with the name of a popular hotel in a small town in the heart of Snowdonia – a place where, shortly before the outbreak of war, we had last met. He had been summoned to Chittagong for a briefing of combined operations prior to the seaborne attack on Akyab, an island off the Arakan coast. The idea that a St David's Day celebration should be arranged was his, whilst I, in anticipation of at least a short period of sick leave after my attack of dysentery, impetuously volunteered to organize the event.

We parted with not too clear a notion of how to proceed, but full of cheerful optimism.

Most of the following month was spent visiting military and air force establishments known to contain Welsh personnel. Enthusiasm for the suggested celebration was unbridled, indeed the war in the Far East could easily have ground to an inglorious standstill on the first day of March, had the allocation of leave passes not been strictly controlled.

A celebratory dinner was eventually held at Cox Bazaar under the unconstitutional title of 'Cymdeithas Cymraeg Godra Burma' (The Burma Frontier Welsh Society), a name decided upon at the inaugural meeting in Chittagong.

Regrettably, the traditionally important leek was not available in Bengal, so the onion soup had to be fancifully described on the menu as 'leek broth!' The chicken and the pudding courses were appropriately referred to by their Welsh equivalents.

By our shameless exaggeration of the importance of the occasion, a unit of the Bombay Sappers and Miners were prevailed upon to donate part of their monthly allocation of army rum to the dinner, and the RAF kindly provided a container.

In the days leading up to the first of March, a preliminary tasting of the rum disclosed it to be heavily impregnated with the taste of high-octane. After a succession of intoxicatingly tedious experiments, it was made tolerably palatable by the addition of a generous squeeze of minty toothpaste to each cupful. I believe we bought up the whole native supply of dentifrice for this purpose.

By popular opinion the occasion was a great success; the meal adjudged better than would have been provided by our respective messes, and the rum potentially good anti-mosquito repellent!

Inevitably we sang our way through a long repertoire of Welsh hymns and arias before departing for our billets in a state of acute nostalgia.

The birth and demise of the Burma Frontier Welsh Society were almost contemporaneous, scarcely long enough for a reluctant expatriate Welsh Dragon to get used to the taste of sulphur in its nostrils.

Throughout the remaining months of 1943 the Arakan was the scene of many bloody battles.

Early in the New Year the battle of the Admin. Box was fought before heavy reinforcements had to be rushed to Assam, where Japanese forces were appearing in strength, as a prelude to their ambitious 'March on Delhi'. It was a time of total commitment for the whole XIVth Army.

When the opening shots in the crucial battle for Imphal and Kohima were fired it was the eve of another St David's Day. 1 March 1944 passed unnoticed – sorry, St David!

Major-General R. E. Lloyd

In early August 1944 the Germans on the front of 59th Infantry Division (of which I was the GSO 1) started their withdrawal towards the River Orne southwards of Villers Bocage.

Things being temporarily slack at Div. HQ my batman and I sallied forth in my jeep to see how our forward troops were faring. We drove through an apparently deserted countryside down a narrow, leafy lane wondering where the enemy (and our own troops) had gone. Suddenly a German helmet, followed by a German head and shoulders, rose from a meadow a hundred yards to our right front, peered in our direction, and sank back into the ground. 'Enemy troops behind our front line; this will never do,' I thought. The lane was too narrow to turn the jeep in, so we walked back and roused a grumpily sleepy infantry section from their cosy billet in a barn. Memories of pre-D-Day battle drill prompted me to suggest that they should lend me a Bren gun with which to indicate the enemy position, distract him, and give covering fire from the left flank while the section attacked straight ahead. Soon we had a nervous but happy prisoner who was led in triumph to my jeep.

The point, if any, of this ridiculous story is that I had put three rounds through its radiator! It did, however, get us back to Div. HQ and our prisoner into the hands of our own Field Security Section . . . Moral for staff officers: 'Don't abandon good intentions merely because they *may* lead you to make yourself look foolish.'

Field-Marshal Sir Richard Hull

In preparing for Operation Torch (North African landing) my regiment (17th/21st Lancers) were practising with the early tank landing craft and living on board a P & O liner on the Clyde. Coming back to the liner in the dark, and with only minimum navigation lights, as the last TLC came alongside a voice was heard say, 'One more bump and my boat would have been head of the river.'

*

Just before the Rhine crossing I was commanding 5th Division and brought it from Italy to BAOR. Monty flew to Ghent to see us, and I was at the airfield to meet him. As the door of his

Dakota opened he looked down at me.

'You are Hull?'

'Yes, sir.'

'A cavalryman?'

'Yes, sir.'

'Commanding an infantry brigade?'

'Yes, sir.'

'Never could have in my army!'

I turned to my ADC and said, 'My size is 6⅞, I'll have a brown one for otter hunting.'

Brigadier J. F. Rickett

The border between Ulster and Eire is well known for smuggling. While I was on a four-month emergency tour in South Armagh I was interested to see that one particular farmer in the south appeared to be digging a tunnel. We kept this under observation for some considerable time and when it was completed the farmer was asked what exactly he was trying to achieve. 'Ach,' he replied, 'I have been told that I cannot smuggle my pigs over the border so I thought I would bring them through underneath instead.'

In the closing stages of the British presence in Aden a few notable Arabs, some of whom were in the federal forces, had defected to Egypt. To my amazement, one of my closest Arab friends, who was serving in the same federal battalion as I was, was one of these. We used to shoot chukar and pigeons together and generally had a lot of fun. He had once called me a blood brother and I felt sad and rather depressed when he disappeared one day without explanation or warning. News came from other sources that he was in Cairo and doing well there.

Some six months later I was down in Aden having dinner, when a scruffy piece of paper landed on my plate with the writing 'Good to see you brother', signed Mohammed. I looked round and saw a prosperous grinning face. After greeting each other warmly I asked him how he had the nerve to show his face again. He replied with an enigmatic grin, 'I went, I saw, I conquered, I did not like, so I returned.'

Later he proceeded to resume his duties in the federal forces without anybody appearing to be surprised or even noticing his absence. Shocked as I was by his perfidy, I could not help laughing at his apparently total lack of guilt or shame. We soon resumed our shooting expeditions.

My tour in south Arabia came to an end all too soon and I returned to England after we had made many promises of keeping in touch. I never saw him again but heard that he was serving with the rebel forces in exile in Saudi Arabia. I heard from him once, a letter I could not answer. It simply said, 'Dear John, do you remember when we were as brothers and used to shoot pigeon together? How is your father and family? Yours, Mohammed. PS. Please send me a self-loading rifle.'

*

It was well known in the Aden protectorate that the local Arab forces used to fiddle their ammunition returns. Any spare ammunition they had usually fell into the hands of the dissidents. One evening I was staying with the federal national guard up country when the fort came under small arms fire. The force inside turned out to a man and returned fire but in the opposite direction. When I pointed out that they were firing 180° the wrong way, I was told, 'That is only Corporal Ahmed who is on leave, we don't want to kill him. Besides, the more ammo we use the more we get given back by the government.'

★

Looting or 'razzing' was quite common at Port Stanley after hostilities had ceased. My battalion was moved into the town and I was appointed commander of all units in the area. I gave clear directions that in future all looted food and equipment should be handed in to the Ordnance Company. While I was walking around Stanley late one evening, I discovered a suspicious, furtive, even shifty, band of men in the depths of some garage, loading stores on to their Land-Rover. Believing that I had caught some looters redhanded, I shouted, 'What are you all doing? Don't you realize that all enemy stores and equipment must be handed in to the Ordnance Company?'

'We *are* the Ordnance Company,' came the reply!

Lord Fanshawe of Richmond

British soldier wounded in New Guinea during the Second World War woke up in an Australian hospital.

Asks: 'Am I going to die?'

Australian nurse replies: 'No. You only arrived yesterday.'

★

Roman Catholic officer cadet being interviewed at Sandhurst. Officer checking interest in alcohol tried to catch cadet out:

'What is Haig?'
'C-in-C Allied Armies (western front).'
'What is Booth?'
'General – Salvation Army.'
'What is Gordon?'
'General killed in Khartoum.'
'What is VAT 69?'
The cadet hesitated and replied, 'Vatican telephone number.'

★

General Eisenhower arrived in Soho, London, during the last war. Pavements were blocked by ladies of the street. 'What is this?' he asked. 'A jam of tarts?'

His English ADC replied: 'No sir, a volume of Trollope's or a line of English pros.'

The Right Honourable
James Callaghan
Member of Parliament

When the Japanese were attacking in Burma, 'Bill' Slim (who was a soldier's general) was always anxious to be up in the front line if he could. At one point, he was told that there were three advance posts closer to the Japanese positions, and he asked to see them. An Indian major was deputed to go with him and at dusk they stumbled forward to the first advance post. When they reached it, the Indian major whispered to Bill Slim, giving him the details of the number of men and machine guns at the post. They then went forward to the second advance post where, once again, the Indian major whispered the information about men and arms. From there they proceeded to the third advance post, closest to the Japanese lines. Bill Slim, in turn, whispered to the Indian major, 'How far away are the Japanese lines?' The Indian major whispered in reply:

'About two thousand yards or so.'

Bill Slim: 'Then why are we whispering?'

Indian major: 'I do not know why, sir, you are whispering, but I have laryngitis.'

Major-General Sir John Acland

A general was visiting the trenches in the First World War and was standing behind a trench occupied by a Guardsman Grant, when a German sniper fired and the bullet whizzed past the general's head.

The general said, 'Good heavens!'

The commanding officer said, 'Shoot him, Grant.'

The regimental sergeant major said, 'Kill him, laddie.'

And Grant fired and from out of a distant tree fell dead a German sniper.

The general said, 'Good God!'

The commanding officer said, 'Well done, young man.'

The regimental sergeant major said, 'Good shot, Grant.'

And Grant said, 'Serve the bugger right for missing the general.'

★

In 1946 I joined as a recruit at the guards depot and subsequently went to the Training Battalion at Pirbright where potential officers were, quite rightly, put through a far more demanding four months' training than that undergone by ordinary recruits. (What a pity it is that such training is not demanded of officer candidates today, particularly the university entrants!)

Though most of the time was spent on field training or endurance, there was, occasionally, on a Saturday morning, a commanding officer's drill parade. One particular Saturday, prior to the parade, our platoon commander, Lieutenant (now Major-General Sir John) Swinton, gave a lecture on the duties of an inspecting officer, emphasizing that it was *only* the inspecting officer who could 'take a man's name' for some fault in turnout, and that other officers or NCOs following behind were never so to do. We received this information with rapt attention, scarcely noticing the wolfish smile on the face of our platoon sergeant, that great Scots guardsman, Sergeant (now Lt-Col. [QM] retd) Donald Whyte.

Shortly after, on parade, we waited in the usual state of trepidation for the inspecting officer, Lt Swinton, who moved down the front rank where I stood and passed me. I sighed with relief. A second or two later Sgt Whyte stopped before me, his face a few inches from mine. His voice came in a terrifying hiss, 'You think the officer's passed you, don't you?'

'Yes, sergeant.'

'You're quite right, he has; but I haven't. What's that on your rifle?'

I glanced down. 'D-d-dust, sergeant?' I asked doubtfully.

The sergeant's voice rose to a scream. 'Dust, my arse. It's rust, red rust. Put him in the guard room, Corporal Lea.'

So I was doubled off parade and incarcerated in a cell. I seethed with rage as the hours passed. That night, the one precious night we got off each fortnight, I was due in London to meet what was, at that time, a very special girl and I couldn't even let her know I could not come. At about 8.00 p.m., when all chance of getting there had gone, Corporal Lea appeared, said I was to be released into open arrest, and that Sergeant Whyte wished to see me. I was marched to his bunk where the great man reclined on his bed, listening to the wireless and appreciatively smoking a Woodbine. I entered and crashed to attention.

'Relax, laddie,' he said quite gently, 'and I'll tell you something. Things have been going a bit too easily for you so you need to learn that life is not fair. If you get a grip of that fact now, you'll do all right. If you don't, God help you. And now,' his voice rose to its paradeground scream, 'turn to your right, fall out and clean your — kit!'

It was the best lesson I've ever been taught because it removed for ever the wholly useless emotion of feeling sorry for oneself.

General Sir Nigel Bagnall
Chief of the General Staff

My wife and I once attended an evening performance of *The Queens and Kings of England* put on by the local dramatic society where I was stationed in Germany. The room was long, the ceiling low, the voices high and our seats distanced from the improvised stage. My hearing was not up to the occasion. As a result, my thoughts and inclinations became increasingly attracted by the prospect of a drink during the interval. The moment arrived and we joined the throng in a neighbouring room. Here somebody approached me and, I thought, asked whether I would like a cup of tea. Somewhat taken aback, I replied that I could not stand the stuff, not at any rate at that hour of the evening. My wife, always alert for such situations, though some feet distant, quickly intervened to explain that the person to whom I was talking was the producer, and what he had asked me was whether the play 'was my cup of tea'.

Major-General John Frost

During the early days of the last war, there was a garrison at Mersa Matruh near the Egyptian frontier with Libya, which was then an Italian colony.

The garrison kept in touch with Middle East HQ in Cairo by wireless, and as there were few urgent signals the contents of the routine messages were left to the signal officers to initiate. One day an inspecting officer asked to see the log of the messages sent and he was a little perturbed to find that the text of the one emanating from Mersa Matruh was nearly always: 'Bullshit makes the grass grow green.' The inspecting officer said, 'Well, that may be true, but surely the initiating officer could show more imagination. I intend to check the log more often in future and I will expect an improvement.'

Two days later he called for the routine message, which now read:

It is lovely here in Mersa Matruh.
The sea and the sky they both are blue.
May the Good Lord bless both the King and the Queen.
But I still say that bullshit makes grass grow green.

★

In the Aldershot Command, between the two world wars, there was a company commander called Captain Scuttle of the Blankshires who had developed a foolproof formula for evading the attentions of senior officers who wished to know what his company was doing when they came to visit him and his company on the training areas.

Whenever he saw the senior officer approaching, he would leap on to his horse and when the officer asked about his companions' activities he would say breathlessly, 'I am afraid that I simply have not time to tell you,' with which he would gallop off into the blue.

One day the elusive company commander's CO and brigadier, who had grown restive with this treatment, decided to make a determined attempt to pin him down. So they planned a pincer movement to surprise Captain Scuttle. As if warned by a sixth sense, our gallant captain called for his horse, which he hastily mounted and, as his two superiors came within earshot, he shouted to his second-in-command: 'Meet me at the rendezvous!'

His second-in-command yelled back, 'But where is the rendezvous?'

Without hesitation came Captain Scuttle's response as he galloped away: 'I simply haven't time to tell you.'

Colonel H. W. R. Pike

Parachute soldiers expect an operation to start with a landing – from the air or the sea. This is what parachutists are taught in their training – but it can backfire. When I was commanding Territorial Army soldiers of The Parachute Regiment in the East Midlands, one of our recruits was a bus driver from Lincoln. On his final night-descent to qualify for his parachute wings, I put him as number one in the 'stick', to give him an easy jump. Unfortunately, the aircraft navigator miscalculated (trust the crabs!), and started dropping us too early. As a result, this unfortunate volunteer found himself descending into a housing estate on the edge of Cranwell airfield. He hit the roof of a house and slid towards 'terra firma', but his parachute hooked itself over the chimney of the house, leaving him dangling ten feet above the back garden, alive and kicking, but shaken and helpless. The back door of the house flew open, and a girl, who transpired to be the 'sitter', emerged. 'You've woken up the baby!' she yelled at the struggling figure. Then she retired, slamming the door, and took no further part in the rescue of the unhappy man.

Could this, I wondered, *really* be a regular occurrence at number 10 Airfield Lane?

*

When I was with 3 Para in Guiana (then British Guiana) some years ago, I led a patrol for several weeks in the area of the

Venezuelan border, along the Wenamu River. My orders stressed one thing above all others – on pain of death would anyone set foot on Venezuelan soil.

We flew to the border in an old Grumman flying boat, and put down on a long disused landing pool on the fast flowing Cuyuni River – one bank of which was Guiana, the other Venezuela. There was no sign of the boat and guide which had been arranged for us, and so the pilot needed to tie up on the bank to offload us. Unfamiliar with the geography, he could find nowhere safe and suitable on the 'home' bank. We therefore chugged across in the Grumman to the only suitable-looking sandbank, and offloaded ourselves and all our kit to start the patrol – on Venezuelan soil. The plan had not survived, though luckily there was no 'contact with the enemy'.

*

It should have been dark – but it was broad daylight, with geese honking and wading birds screaming. The young lions of 3 Para were all 'raring to go', as the landing craft (belonging to the Royal Marines and therefore known disparagingly by parachutists as 'rubbish tips') cut through the calm, sunlit waters towards Sand Bay. Every soldier had imagined such a moment as this throughout his career – the ramp slamming down, the aggressive rush for the shore, the fight up the beach, the bridgehead established, the enemy savaged and put to flight.

Still some hundred yards out, and in water too deep to wade, the landing craft 'bellied' on the bottom, backed off, tried again, bellied again. Packed tightly and laden with ammunition, we waited helplessly while one of the crew climbed along the side of the craft, testing the depth of the water with a long white pole. 'F— me, sir,' said Sergeant Chris Phelan beside me, 'We've got a blind man in charge now.' After several more

92

attempts to nudge the landing craft on to the beach, we transferred to a smaller landing craft with a shallower draft, cruised into the beach, and waded ashore thankful that our morning's boating was over. The enemy missed witnessing our discomfort, though their aircraft found us soon afterwards. But perhaps even if they had been there, they'd have joined in the fun and killed themselves laughing.

*

The adjutant was having a bad morning, and had been plagued recently by a fellow officer who was something of a practical joker. The telephone rang. 'Is that the adjutant? Ah, good morning, it's the Field-Marshal speaking . . . '

' . . . Oh, do b— off, Roger,' interjected the adjutant, 'I've got work to do,' and he replaced the receiver firmly.

Monty got a different response when he rang the commanding officer a short time afterwards!

General Sir Frank Kitson

On one occasion in Northern Ireland an officer had been invited to a dinner to mark the 200th anniversary of some blood-stained event which was evidently of considerable local significance. He had been asked to say a few words after the meal.

'As the time for his speech approached he became aware of the fact that several other prominent persons had also been asked to make a similar contribution to the evening's entertainment, one of whom was sitting on his right. This man spoke first and the officer was surprised and annoyed to find that his neighbour was making precisely the speech which he had planned to make. Indeed, he soon noticed that his neighbour was reading from his own text which was lying in front of him on the table. A final annoyance was that despite the elegance of his speech and the fluency with which his neighbour read it, he received very little applause.

The officer was then called upon to make his contribution and, being reluctant to impose his speech on the diners a second time, he cast around in his mind for something to say. For an awful moment he could think of nothing, but then he caught sight of the menu and went through it course by course suitably embellishing each French phrase with a few thoroughly English comments. In doing so he brought the house down.

Later he discovered that his neighbour was head of the catering firm which had arranged the dinner.

Lieutenant-Colonel
C. P. B. Keeble

The importance of precision in the use of English in service writing has always been stressed in the education of the staff officer. An instructor at the Staff College wishing to illustrate the point, told the story of the elderly couple who had known each other many years, and, to avoid running two households, had decided to get married.

They discussed the matter carefully, covering all the points except one! The elderly lady broached the subject by asking ' . . . and what about sex?'

'Infrequently,' replied the man.

'Yes, my dear,' said the lady, 'but, is that one word or two?'

★

The crisis situation such as one finds on the battlefield produces a brand of mirth known as 'black humour'. The Falklands Campaign had its stockpile of such jokes.

The ink was hardly dry on John Nott's famous Defence White Paper, which proposed a largely sub-surface navy at the expense of the surface fleet when the Falklands Campaign started.

After the amphibious landing, Lieutenant-Colonel H. Jones, Commanding Officer of 2 Para, was standing amid his battalion's position on Sussex Mountain, taking in the frightful aftermath of the savage Argentine air attacks on the surface ships in and around the beachhead of San Carlos. Numerous ships had been hit and many were burning. For the soldiers it was their first taste of the Falklands conflict and many were shocked. 'H' (who had a brother in the navy), brightened the gloom of the spectators when, as he looked at the scene, he quipped, 'John Nott bloody well wanted a sub-surface navy, and it looks as if the Argentine air force have just provided him with one!'

*

During the closing stages of the Battle of Goose Green, a young soldier from the recce platoon was caught on the forward slope of Darwin Hill by devastating fire of the Argentine anti-aircraft guns in the settlement.

As he lay in agony, the shock of the realization of the extent of his injuries suddenly overtook him and he screamed to his section commander, 'Corporal, I've lost my leg.'

His leader, trying to impose his leadership and bring a measure of calm to the crisis of the moment, shouted back, 'It's OK, Gray, keep calm, you haven't lost your bloody leg. I've found it over here!'

*

You have heard of psychological warfare, or 'psyops' as it is more commonly called, in which an attempt is made either to reinforce the strength of will of one's own side, or destroy the will of the enemy, by psychological measures. Lord Haw Haw's broadcasts in the Second World War, or the enticements of Tokyo Rose in the Vietnam War, even the graffiti on the Crumlin Road Jail, are good examples. Sometimes this uncertain branch of warfare has a quite different effect from the desired; and such was the case in the Falklands Campaign.

The Argentine commander had primed his commanders to stiffen the resolve of the 'defenders' around the settlement at Goose Green. 'Tell the soldiers,' he said, 'that the English paratroopers have been ordered to eat their prisoners of war. Ensure the men fight to prevent the positions being captured.'

The threat clearly did not have the desired effect and the positions were lost to 2 Para. The 'psyops', however, had left its mark on the POWs, since we always seemed to elicit more information from the prisoners during tactical questioning if the interrogators had a knife and fork on the table beside him!

*

As the leading section commander of B Coy, 2 Para came under effective .5 machine gun fire on the approach to Goose Green, he was heard to cry frantically into his radio, 'For f—'s sake Scotty, beam me up!'

*

During an important study day at the School of Infantry, the commandant was summing up the major points made during the long session in the humid atmosphere of the Blenheim Hall. For one student, near the front row, the struggle to stay awake

96

had been too great, and his eyelids closed, and his jaw sagged.

The sight of the sleeping student was too much for the general. He raged at the student's neighbour, 'You there, wake up that man on your right!'

'No sir,' came the brave reply. 'You sent him to sleep, you wake him up!'

*

There are many stories about those pen pictures written in officers' confidential reports, from 'his men would follow him anywhere, if only out of curiosity' to the cryptic career-stopping phrase for one cavalry subaltern, 'I wouldn't breed from this officer!' My favourite is the neat solution provided by the commanding officer, who was being berated by an injured party. 'I object, sir, to the word "drunk" in the phrase "this officer is sometimes drunk" in my report.' The erudite leader glanced at the report for a second, and said, 'I agree with you,' picked up his pen, crossed out the offending word, and replaced it with the word 'sober'!

Brigadier H. M. Rose

A soldier was walking along the road in a barracks which his regiment shared with the RAF. An air commodore wearing a combat jacket and an unimpressive side hat, a form of dress which gave little hint of his exalted rank, walked past in the opposite direction and was ignored. Turning, he demanded, 'You! Don't you salute air commodores in the Queen's Own Highlanders?' The soldier stared at him for a second, considering the question carefully, before smiling sweetly and

97

answering, 'Noo sir, we dinna *have* air commodores in the Queen's Own Highlanders!'

*

A recently promoted brigadier from the Guards had just arrived in the Middle East to take command of a brigade, which consisted mostly of Arab soldiers under command of British officers on secondment. On his initial tour of inspection of an Armoured Car Regiment, the brigadier, who had a keen eye for detail and was known to demand high standards of dress and turn out, peered into the interior of one of the armoured cars. Looking none too pleased with what he had seen, he turned to the young fresh-faced English Cavalry officer standing beside him and snapped, 'There are far too many flies in this vehicle,' to which the troop commander languidly responded, 'How many would you like there to be, sir?'

*

Over the years the British Army in Northern Ireland had been subjected to a great many complaints regarding the state of a football pitch which lay alongside one of their South Armagh bases. The soldiers in the base had tried their hardest not to interfere with the activities of the local club and had gone to great lengths to meet all the various requests made to them. Having at last thought that no reason could possibly exist for further complaint, they had been surprised to be summoned to yet another meeting with the club where on this occasion they were accused of having tunnelled beneath the football pitch. When the company commander in command of the base asked why the members of the club thought that this was happening, the chairman of the club replied, 'Whenever one of our players lands on his head, he hears a hollow ring!'

General
Sir Anthony Farrar-Hockley

In the very earliest days of military parachuting during the war, the British Army drew in volunteers piecemeal; but this was soon seen to involve many administrative difficulties. So it was arranged that existing battalions should be converted, the volunteers among them remaining as a body for training while others came in from outside to fill out to full establishment.

The Royal Air Force were responsible for basic parachute training. They found the Army strange, not least in such matters as regimental loyalty and formal discipline, but while they were dealing with drafts of men as individuals they felt able to bend them temporarily to Royal Air Force ways. Suddenly they had to cope with the training of a formed battalion under its own commanding officer.

I served in the first such battalion to arrive at No. 1 Parachute Training School, Ringway (now Manchester Airport). My commanding officer, renowned before the war as a wild subaltern (he had won a bet that he could dine in Paris on the day that he was orderly officer in Gravesend without missing a single parade), had responded to the stern demands of war by becoming a stickler for duty. He would not have, for example, his officers and soldiers strolling casually to training parades in the hangar, dressed in a variety of military clothing. We were the better for the standards he set and his dynamic energy in pursuing them. But our Royal Air Force instructors regarded him as a smoking grenade, dangerous but demanding respect.

During the early days of ground training, the Royal Air Force ceased trying to bend the Army to its ways and learned to adapt to the latter's peculiarities.

We reached the morning of the first parachute descent. It was quiet and sunny. Soldiers, airmen and the great barrage balloon from whose dangling basket we were about to leap into space, were all met precisely on time. The balloon ascended. My commanding officer made the first jump, setting us all an example.

The chief instructor was in charge on the dropping zone. As each man jumped, he abated their terrors as they descended with a soothing critique. 'Well done, number 2, good exit, get your feet and knees together. You're really going to enjoy your landing.'

'I now feel,' the chief instructor remarked to his assistants, 'that we have reached a mutual understanding with the Army. They have stopped surprising us.'

He should never have said those words. The commanding officer had picked himself up and was watching number 2 now immediately above him in the air, ready to 'enjoy' his landing. Suddenly he stiffened and pointed angrily upwards.

'Arrest that man!' he cried to the regimental sergeant major. 'No studs in his boots.'

Major-General D. T. Crabtree

A padre who had been finding life on his salary very difficult, especially since he had five children to bring up and educate, decided to have a word with God. Having established contact he said: 'Tell me, Lord, is it true that in your eyes ten thousand years is like unto a twinkling of an eye?'

'Yes, that is true, my son.'

100

'And Lord, is it also true that a million pounds would be like unto you a penny?'

'Yes, my son, you could say that.'

'Well, Lord, do you think you could possibly let me have a penny?'

'Yes, of course, my son, but could you just give me a minute to arrange it?'

Brigadier R. M. B. Walker

I suppose that pipers, in common with other musicians, like an appreciative audience, and I was certainly naive enough to think so on that September morning in Jakarta in 1963, the day the new state of Malaysia was born.

I had arrived some months previously as a young, eager assistant military attaché, as the War Office in its wisdom clearly foresaw 'confrontation' looming and the situation in the region deteriorating. I was welcomed as a useful member of the diplomatic staff. Little did they know!

My information, passed discreetly by some Indonesian friends, was that a few unruly characters, primed by government propaganda, were being organized to pay us a visit, just to make clear President Sukarno's attitude to Malaysia and our contribution in bringing it about. Surely, I thought, a tune or two could only add a little something to the atmosphere!

At around 1030 hours, the first demonstrators arrived in the square between the embassy and the Hotel Indonesia, the inhabitants of which were taking their seats for what was billed as an interesting spectacle.

The crowd, coming now in their hundreds, pushed up against the embassy perimeter until the railings were lined by a jeering, shouting, gesticulating mob, stretching far back into the square. Surely this must be the moment for a tune – and quickly, too.

The mob ringleader, standing on the top of the gatepost with his loudhailer, paused in mid-sentence, and for a moment, as the chanting of the crowd died away, the sound of the 'Cameron Men' wafted across the square to those enjoying the spectacle from the hotel vantage point – not to mention the diplomats locked inside the embassy. Alas, I must have played a bum note, for soon well over three thousand voices shouted their appreciation, emphasized by a shower of bricks and stones. Luckily, I had kept close to the railings as I marched up and down, thus spoiling the aim of those in the front rank and the majority of the fusillade passed harmlessly overhead. It was only later, with fine tactical sense, that they tore down the railings! The building had only been in commission for some thirteen months and, following the design of that period, was made with temptingly large areas of glass – a rioter's delight. They took full advantage of it.

I suppose the whole affair lasted some twenty to thirty minutes, and, quite apart from the ambassador's car and the Union flag being ceremonially burned, I long remember the military attaché, who throughout this extraordinary affair stood alone, outside the building, complete with monocle. His face betrayed annoyance and on occasions a look of agony, undoubtedly attributable to my playing, which by this time was unlikely to be of competition standard. The ambassador, a seasoned campaigner from Wartime Special Forces, had already been under similar harassment when 'our man' in Iceland. Indeed, the press credited him with playing the pipes on that occasion but, although a man of many parts and pungent wit, he lays no claim to playing the great highland war pipe.

As the years passed the story of Jakarta has grown in the telling and is still cited by the Foreign Office as a prime example of the army 'out of control'. However, some years after confrontation was over, I happened to be stationed in Singapore. A new embassy had arisen from the ashes of the old one, for indeed the mob had returned two days after the stoning with instructions to burn us out. They did just that. The grand reopening in 1968 was clearly to be regarded as a turning point in British-Indonesian relations. 'You must come over for the ceremony,' said my Indonesian friends, who love a good joke. 'Provocation,' murmured the Foreign Office, whose sense of humour, and judgement, I have at times regarded as a little suspect. So there was no return to Jakarta – that is, until August 1984 when, a free man at last on retirement, I visited Indonesia once again. It was delightful in every way; but a moment I shall long relish came after the inevitable 'battlefield tour' of the premises with the current ambassador. Very much a Far East hand, with a decided twinkle, he quietly asked me whether perhaps I had a photograph of 'the incident' to hang in the corridor as a memento of this interesting period of embassy history.

Most certainly I had – and it's there now.

Field-Marshal Sir John Stanier

A distinguished officer of the Household Division made a great name for himself in his youth when, as adjutant of his battalion, he inspired fear into the hearts of all by his meticulous standards on the drill square.

On one particular morning on which both the adjutant and the regimental sergeant major had occasion to inspect the parade, a young officer emerged late from the officers' mess building and ran on to the parade ground to take his place on the square.

The adjutant, eyeing this development with some displeasure, invited the sergeant major to give his compliments to the unfortunate young officer and invite him to wait upon the adjutant at his office.

When the young man presented himself, the adjutant spoke to him as follows: 'In the Grenadier Guards, Mr Smyth, we are never late. Therefore, Mr Smyth, in the Grenadier Guards there is never a requirement to run. Indeed, Mr Smyth, it is not enough merely to walk. In the Grenadier Guards, Mr Smyth, we should always walk *sumptuously*.'

Airy Tales

Group Captain G. R. Profitt

It was Christmas Eve one year in the early 1920s and a fighter squadron decided to celebrate the occasion by overflying the airfield of a rival squadron and dropping festive loo rolls. This was done to great effect. On New Year's Eve the rival squadron decided to retaliate. They went down to the airfield pig farm and filled a large sack with the ripest of pig manure. This was then balanced precariously on the side of the squadron commander's open cockpit and he took off to 'bomb' the other squadron's airfield. His navigation and bomb-aiming were immaculate and the sack exploded with a satisfying plop in front of the rival squadron's headquarters. On landing back at his own airfield, the squadron commander was puzzled to find the station commander, the chaplain and most of his squadron standing in an anxious group holding a signal message. They cheered up considerably when he climbed from his aircraft and then showed him the signal. It was from the squadron he had just bombed and it read: 'We regret to inform you that during a practice bomb attack on our airfield this morning, your squadron commander fell from his aircraft and received fatal injuries'!

The Right Honourable
James Molyneaux
Member of Parliament

Shortly after the end of the Second World War my wing commander 'acquired' a young Luftwaffe NCO to serve as his batman. Hans spoke fairly good English and, being anxious to behave correctly, sought the advice of the adjutant and me as to how he ought to respond to the CO's thanks for his morning tea. I suggested that Hans might click his heels, stand to attention and say, 'Our day will come.'

The adjutant and I peered through the flap of our tent next morning and watched Hans fleeing across the orchard, followed by a tray, a teacup and a naked wing commander brandishing his revolver. We thought it only right to own up; a forgiving Hans was reinstated and peace broke out again.

The Right Honourable
Merlyn Rees
Member of Parliament

In the interwar years the battle for an independent air force was won. After the fall of France in 1940, however, a rethinking had to take place on practical cooperation between the army and the RAF on the western desert battlefield. In 1942 the first practical exercises in the field took place, albeit with too many paper units controlling fictional aircraft.

In 1943 after a more real exercise in southern England those of us in No. 1 Mobile Operations Room Unit (MORU) found ourselves in a convoy of ships sailing out of the Atlantic into the Mediterranean, bound for where?

In early June we were huddled together in the hold of a 'troopship', fully dressed in battle dress, heavy boots in a temperature of about 100°F, waiting to get into LSTs either down the nets or by deft jumps! We were off Sicily and not, as we were beginning to think from our clothing, the Arctic Circle. Italian aircraft had shot quickly over our heads at first light and missed us widely with their bombs. At least we had arrived.

Soon we were off for the shore – the officers armed with

Smith and Wessons in one hand and suitcases in the other. The beachmasters – desert-booted, scruffy-hatted, silk-scarved, long-haired officers of the Eighth Army – shepherded us quickly up on to the road almost disdainfully.

We walked in small groups, Indian file, crossed the rutted-by-tanks 'main road' and up the hill to Mellilli, en route for Lentini. It was to be a long trek with our friends from the infantry – and we were in the *air* force.

As we proceeded I heard one of our lads cry out plaintively, ''E promised us blood, sweat and tears and he was right. My feet are bleeding, I'm sweating buckets and I can't see through the dust and the tears!' And so it went on through Salerno, Anzio and the south of France. Thus was army/air cooperation strengthened to reach its culminating point in Western Europe.

Air Commodore J. M. Pack

At a Vulcan bomber station in Lincolnshire during the sixties, the station commander decided that the time was right for him to have a purge on general discipline. Amongst other measures designed to tighten up what he considered to be a gradual loosening of standards and behaviour, he ordered all officers to charge, on the spot, any airman who failed to salute or to pay the proper alternative respects. I was in my car, in uniform, and had just turned on to the main road into Lincoln when I passed an airman, also in uniform, standing on the side of the road clearly hoping for a lift. As I moved away from the T-junction I passed him very slowly and, whilst he stared at me, and I at him, he made no effort whatever to salute. Remembering my station commander's directive, I came to an abrupt halt and jumped out of the car. However, before I could get out even one word of my mentally prepared 'Are you blind? Don't you normally salute officers when you recognize them?' etc., he had jumped into the back seat of the car and was in the process of thanking me for stopping, telling me that anywhere in Lincoln would do, and that it was not really necessary for me to get out – he could cope with getting in quite well on his own!

Clearly, I should have gathered my somewhat shocked wits and proceeded with the charge; I didn't – speechless, I dropped him, as he requested, in the centre of Lincoln.

★

On a quiet Sunday evening, a very young and junior officer entered the bar in his mess to find only one other person there; an elderly, well-dressed, distinguished-looking gentleman whom he did not know. With youthful enthusiasm, the youngster introduced himself and explained that he had just heard a tremendously good new joke about navigators and was bursting to tell someone. The elderly gentleman responded very coolly, but, despite his displayed indifference, was quite unable to put off the young pilot. In some desperation, the distinguished visitor finally raised his voice and successfully stopped the youngster who was into the first few words of his new joke: 'Before you go any further, young man, you would wish to know that I am a serving Air Marshal and, moreover, that I am a navigator.'

Without hesitation, and still bubbling with irrepressible enthusiasm to tell his joke, the young pilot responded: 'Oh, OK sir, I'll tell it *very* slowly,' and continued!

Air Marshal Sir Michael Knight

A large tent had been pitched among the foothills of the Aden hinterland, to serve as a temporary mess for army and RAF officers engaged in the protection of the national interest, as then perceived. Very early one morning a solitary figure was taking breakfast – a subaltern of a famous regiment, who had been appointed duty officer for the day and who, by custom, was therefore arrayed in full service dress uniform – including hat. He was reading a three-week-old copy of the *Telegraph* – the latest available. Enter two rather less elegantly attired young RAF pilots, on their return from a dawn reconnaissance sortie – very hot and decidedly less than fresh in their already sodden flying suits. They sat down at the table and duly ordered from the Arab steward the standard aircrew breakfast of bacon and fried eggs, tomato, sausage, baked beans and fried bread. Their cheery morning greeting to their army colleague appeared to have gone unheard, for he was still immersed in his newspaper as he toyed delicately with a bowl of cereal.

In due course came the aircrew breakfast, and one of the young pilots enquired of the back of the newspaper whether the army officer might pass the salt. There was no response – nor, indeed, a flicker of recognition on the slightly louder repeat of the request. However, at the third time of asking, the duty officer wearily laid down his paper and said: 'You RAF chaps obviously don't understand the custom of my regiment. When a chap is sitting in the mess wearing his hat, it means that he wishes neither to speak nor to be spoken to,' and he again disappeared behind the *Telegraph*.

One of the young airmen rose, walked around the table to stand behind the army officer, unlaced a desert flying boot and dropped it carefully into the bowl of cornflakes. Infuriated soldier leaps to his feet, demanding an explanation. 'Oh it's simple, old chap,' said the pilot. 'You chaps obviously don't understand the custom of the Royal Air Force. When a chap drops his flying boot into another chap's cornflakes, it means "Pass the — salt!" '

*

Three lifelong friends (amazingly, an admiral, a general and an air marshal) were brought to a sudden and simultaneous end when their aircraft hit a mountain – thus effectively interrupting the rather heated discussion they were having as to the relative importance of the three armed services.

To the slight surprise of one, and the blank astonishment of the others, they found themselves on the glittering pathway to the gates of Heaven, and decided that, as discord must for them be a thing of the past, they had better establish, for their eternal peace of mind, whether a view was held in heaven on such matters as interservice status. St Peter was only too pleased to help.

'Indeed,' said he, 'God has pronounced on that very subject only today.' And to his three newest arrivals he pointed out a wall, fifteen feet high, on which was inscribed, in perfect Gothic script, the words: 'There can be no differentiation as between the relative importance of the three armed services of the British Crown – signed, God.'

However, beneath the signature, and in slightly smaller lettering there appeared: 'Air Commodore (retired)'!

Air Chief Marshal
Sir Peter Harding

An American air force aircraft, flying into Clarkfield AFB in the Philippines, asked for landing instructions. After the instructions had been given the aircraft replied: 'Air Force 249 Roger Dodger.'

TOWER: 'Air Force 249 Roger will be sufficient acknowledgement, over.'

AIRCRAFT: 'Air Force 249 Roger Dodger.'

TOWER: 'Air Force 249, I say again, Roger will be sufficient acknowledgement, over.'

AIRCRAFT: 'Air Force 249 Roger Dodger.'

TOWER (*change of voice*): 'Air Force 249, this is Colonel Lee-White, the senior air traffic control officer, Roger will be sufficient acknowledgement, over.'

AIRCRAFT (*after a long pause*): 'Air Force 249 this is General Schmoltzenheimer, Roger Dodger!'

*

Two Meteor fighters broke into the circuit and landed.
   The first aircraft called, 'Mike Alfa clearing starboard.'
   The second, 'Mike Bravo following suit.'
   The first aircraft, when off the runway, called, 'Suit clear'!

John Courtney

I would like to state, at the very beginning, that all the events described here actually took place. Names of people have been avoided but any similarity between actual persons, living or dead, and those mentioned is purely intentional.

Doubtless many wartime servicemen would have agreed that the second most popular thing on their minds was leave and, like *the* most popular thing, we never seemed to get enough of it. So there were always those of us who were prepared to risk stealing a few precious clandestine hours at home if we thought we could get away with it. But unfortunately the dice were heavily loaded against us. Firstly, 'they' had a nasty habit of sending one hundreds of miles from one's home and then putting a limit of about ten miles on the distance one was allowed to stray from camp. Secondly, 'they' made us wear distinctive uniforms for the sole purpose of spotting us when we were up to something of which 'they' did not approve. Thirdly, and this shows how nasty 'they' really were, a special corps of sadistic clairvoyants was formed who were trained to read one's innermost thoughts and sniff out those who tried to beat the system. These people, who mainly infested railway stations and bus termini and were answerable only to Satan himself, were variously known as NPs (navy), MPs (army), SPs (RAF) and bastards.

Another antisocial group, of equally dubious parentage, was that tribe of officers and NCOs who were fanatically dedicated to leave-stopping. Fighter pilots painted little swastikas on their machines to show the number of enemy planes they had shot down; bomber crews painted little white bombs on the noses of their aircraft to indicate the number of raids they had made; these people probably collected cancelled leave passes as trophies. Particularly Scrooge-like was Sergeant Torturer (an unskilled trade of course), who pretended to be deaf when it suited his devious purposes but seemed to hear very well indeed on some occasions: such as when somebody offered to buy him a drink. Officially he was a physical training instructor but, being disgustingly obese and possessed of the voice of a eunuch when he was excited, he was not too successful in that activity. He was also as bald as a coot and fancied himself as a comedian, a pursuit at which he was also rather inept.

Some of us were happily looking forward to a well-earned (official) '48', and had a few little bits and pieces packed ready for departure the following day, when Baldilocks decided to hold his annual PT period (more than once a year would have killed him) and we were detailed to participate. Well, he squeaked and wobbled his way through a routine of sorts, boring us all to tears with his pathetically weak and badly delivered jokes, and as the period dragged on it became clear that he was getting more and more annoyed at those of our derisive comments which managed to penetrate his earwax. The crunch came when he thought somebody had made a disrespectful reference to his hairless dome. 'I'll 'ave you lot know,' he shrilled angrily, 'Grass don't grow on a busy street.' Originality was not his strongest talent. We should have laughed dutifully and let it pass, but it was not to be. Somebody at the back, in an unusually loud stage-whisper said, 'It doesn't grow in a bloody desert either.' This provoked the first genuine laughter of the whole period but, unluckily, the flight sergeant's hearing made one of its inconvenient recoveries at that moment and thus provided him with the opportunity for which he had, no doubt, been waiting. He cancelled our passes.

*

In spite of incidents like that just recounted, I did manage to make a modest contribution to the war effort and enjoy a few legitimate leaves as well. I also enjoyed a few illegitimate leaves when the opportunities presented themselves. The temptations were always greatest when one was posted to a station which was within a reasonable day's travelling from one's home, and I confess to having succumbed a few times. I got away with it most of the time but not because of any great astuteness on my part; in fact there were times when I was incredibly stupid, literally walking into the arms of waiting SPs who were either dafter than me or uncharacteristically human – a possibility I was loath to admit. The following happenings illustrate what I mean.

The processes by which aircrew cadets were turned into pilots, navigators, gunners, etc., were very long-winded. There were many delays in training so that the authorities must have found it extremely difficult to find enough activity to keep us all adequately occupied. We spent many useless and boring weeks waiting for courses. Nobody, staff or inmates, who had the misfortune to be incarcerated for months on end in Stalag Heaton Park near Manchester will ever forget it. In order to relieve this state of affairs some of us were sent on temporary attachment to operational RAF stations to make ourselves useful. I found myself on a bomber station near Cambridge, but since I, like the rest of my group, had no talents as yet in which bomber command were interested, was of very little use. Apart from keeping our quarters clean and running an occasional errand, there was not much for us to do, so while the rest of the station got on with the war we were left to our own devices most of the time.

We soon discovered that the airfield was situated within reasonably walkable distance from one of the main roads into London and hitch-hiking was not difficult for someone in uniform. My home was not far from London so that the situation was tailor-made for what was to become one of my favourite off-duty pastimes – *trying* to slide off home when I would not be missed. There was, of course, the problem of passes, or rather, the lack of them; but this was not a serious disadvantage provided one could dodge the dreaded SPs.

I laid my plans carefully and systematically:

1. Fix it with friends to cover for me if I should be missed.
2. Travel light – shaving kit in gas mask case, nothing else. All other requirements to be found at home; eat in cafés if necessary.
3. Hitch-hike to northern outskirts of London.
4. Travel rest of the way by bus, avoiding termini.
5. Return by reversing the sequence.

Foolproof? What did Robert Burns say about mice and men?

When the opportunity arose for my first trip I got up early and, using a convenient gap in the hedge, left the camp unnoticed. I made my way to the main road where I soon obtained a lift in the back of a London-bound brewer's dray. The driver obligingly dropped me in north London at about 10 a.m. and I then had the bright idea of telephoning my girlfriend at her office to see if she could get the rest of the day off to spend with me. I looked around for a phone booth but there was none in sight. Just across the road was a railway station. 'Aha,' I thought, 'where there are trains there are bound to be telephones.' And so there were. As I entered the station, five empty phone booths were ready and waiting for my convenience, but standing by the end one, in all his detestable regalia, was a gigantic SP.

It was a nasty shock. I could have kicked myself. There must have been other phones about. Why come in here? Twit! I had visions of arrest and being charged with absence without leave, desertion even; the glasshouse; ignominious discharge from the Royal Air Force; and all for a crafty night at home. But then, it seemed to me, the SP was not really interested in me, he was reading a newspaper, so I decided to bluff it out. I walked as calmly as I could towards the booth furthest away from him, and was just about to enter it, when – 'Hey – YOU!' The SP had lowered his paper and was looking hard at me.

'M-me, corporal?'

'Yes, lad, you. Come 'ere.'

With heavy heart and leaden feet I approached. 'I'll never be a pilot now,' I thought miserably, 'I'll be lucky if I come out of this alive.' As I reached him he spoke again. 'Don't use that one, lad, it's out of order. Use this one.' He nodded his head toward the nearest box. Whereupon he turned on his heel and marched smartly away.

*

There was a 'flap' on. Everybody who was of even the slightest importance in the running of the station was called upon for maximum effort. We aircrew cadets, being of no importance at all, and useless to boot, received even less attention than before. We offered help, of course, but we were told, impolitely, to get lost.

The 'flap' was nationwide. All leave was cancelled. Even worse, off-duty travel was restricted to a five-mile radius of camp. We were out of bounds even in Cambridge. Everyone was informed that, in order to enforce the ban, SPs would not only patrol the main rail and bus termini, but the branch networks as well. Even the roads were to be watched. What a challenge! I couldn't resist it.

The usual preparations were made: shaving kit in gas mask case, emergency cover arrangements – all, by now, standard procedures. The only problem was transport; all the usual routes would be lousy with SPs. 'Go by bike,' said someone. 'Fifty odd miles,' I thought, 'why not?' One of my comrades had acquired a ramshackle old bicycle which I persuaded him to lend me, so, as they say, I was in business. It was a hazardous prospect but I had only recently been married and, such is the power of love, I pressed on.

It was a lovely day for a cycle ride and all went well until I was about a mile or so from Buntingford. My back tyre suddenly deflated and I had no means of mending the puncture. I had no choice but to walk, pushing the bicycle. Fortunately I found a shop where they repaired cycles and, although they were too busy to mend my puncture, they did allow me to use their workshop to do it myself. A half-hour later I was on my way again, but my difficulties were not over yet. Some two miles further on I was held up by, of all things, a traffic jam. (Petrol was supposed to be rationed, remember.) Stretching for at least half a mile in front of me was a nose-to-tail queue of vehicles. At this point I was not unduly worried. It is easy with a bicycle to weave one's way forward through stationary traffic, so I was able to reach the front of the queue fairly quickly.

Well, I *hadn't* been worried. There, forming a human barrier across the road, were four men in uniform: a civil policeman, a dirty great chief petty officer, a red-capped MP, and a sergeant SP who were stopping all cars and apprehending all hitch-hikers wearing uniforms. Judging by the size of the group of miserable-looking men and women from all three services standing by the roadside, they were having a field day. I considered turning about and hightailing back to camp, but it was too late; I had obviously been spotted. Once again, I decided to brazen it out. Without waiting to be invited I cycled right up to the sergeant, stopped and said, 'Want me, sarge?' He looked me up and down while I tried to appear as if it was the most natural thing in the world to be cycling down the main road to London during a leave ban. He pointed to my scrapyard steed and asked, 'Going to London?' I did my best to look shocked. 'What?' I replied, 'On this?' He shook his head in disbelief, waved me on and turned his attention to more important matters.

About thirty-six hours later I staggered back into camp at 3.00 a.m., having made it home and back (just). The old bike held up well, although its saddle had seen better days and I had a sore backside for a week afterwards – but it was worth it.

*

'AIRMAN – COME HERE!' The shock of that ear-splitting bellow nearly stopped my heart beating. Some would put it down to my guilty conscience. You see, I should not have been on platform 5 of Euston station at five minutes to midnight on that Sunday. I was on yet another crafty '48', and, being by now an old hand at the game, I knew I would not be missed at camp provided that I was on duty by Monday morning. I knew from experience that the 12.03 a.m. would get me there in good time. But things were going wrong; I was rather more than the approved ten miles from camp (I was stationed near Birmingham at the time), I had no pass, and I had been rumbled. You could say that I was up the well-known creek minus the proverbial paddle.

The irony of it all was that until then I had successfully dodged the SPs at Waterloo, and in the main area of Euston (no mean feat – after all, a craftsman is entitled to be proud of his skill). I had been congratulating myself on having passed safely through the ticket barrier on to the platform itself, which SPs did not, as a rule, haunt. Having mingled with hundreds of other service men and women and almost reached the safety of the train itself, it was a cruel blow to get clobbered at such a late stage.

'AIRMAN – yes, YOU. COME HERE!' Although the blast came from behind, and I was but one of a multitude, I *knew* it was meant for *me*. I turned and saw not one but two of them, and they appeared to be *laughing*. Now SPs are not generally addicted to mirth, so I was, understandably, uneasy. 'Cat and mouse,' I thought, 'I'm the mouse and these bastards are going to play with me before they pounce.' One of them extended a finger and beckoned. Quakingly I complied. At this point I became aware that the crowd was unusually interested in the proceedings; furthermore, there was a general atmosphere of amusement at someone else's discomfort.

'That's right,' I said to myself, 'enjoy the spectacle. If we had a guillotine you'd all be bloody knitting.'

'Where do you think you're going then?' one of them giggled.

'Birmingham, corporal,' I said unhappily.

I knew what came next: he would say, 'Where's yer pass?' and I would say, 'Haven't got one, corporal.' And then out would come the hateful little notebook and pencil which would be given the ritual lick. 'Right then. Name and number? Station? Yoolbeonachargewenyagetthere.' But none of that happened. Instead, he gasped, 'Well put yer bloody 'at on properly lad,' and immediately joined his doubled-up colleague in peals of hysterical laughter which was echoed by the surrounding crowd.

Miserably, I reached to adjust my cap, one of the old 'fore and aft' glengarry type which, according to instructions, was supposed to be worn with the front buttons 'one inch above the right eye'. But the buttons weren't there. With horror I realized that I had travelled all the way from home to Waterloo, across London on a crowded tube train, through the hazards of Euston and almost the entire length of platform 5 with my hat, with its distinctive white flash, back to front. I must have been seen and laughed at by thousands.

'What do I do now, corporal?' I asked, timidly.

'Do?' he yelped. 'Do?' he repeated between guffaws, and

spraying me with fine spittle. 'Get out of my bloody sight.'
I obeyed, smartly. 'Quit while you're ahead,' I thought.

Sir Michael Beetham
Marshal of the Royal Air Force

I trained as a pilot in the Second World War with the US Army
Air Corps in the southern states of America – Florida, Alabama
and Georgia. The flying training was excellent but as cadets we
were subjected to the so-called Honour System born out of
West Point, which has caused much controversy and heart-
searching in the US Forces. Certainly many of its features were
not taken kindly to by the British cadets, who were nevertheless
determined to survive and, in true British tradition, 'beat the
system'.

To try and instil us with their military discipline, part of the
routine at Primary Flying School in Florida involved us being
woken at first light, 0530 hours, by a loud clanging bell, being
on parade in our coveralls five minutes later, while 'The Star
Spangled Banner' was played and the flag raised. We would
subsequently return to wash, shave, dress and have breakfast.
There were 100 cadets all told, a US flight of 50 and an RAF
flight of 50, each under our own cadet officer whose task was to
report us 'all present and correct' to the American staff duty
officer.

None of us in the RAF particularly cared for this early
morning disturbance and, among ourselves, worked out a
system whereby only 40 of us would turn out each day thus
giving each of us one morning off in five, our cadet officer (one
of us) reporting 'all present and correct'.

This subterfuge was not spotted by the American duty officer, but our US friends in the other flight quickly did. Not wanting to upset Anglo-American relations they tackled us with it, saying somewhat sheepishly that under the Honour Code they would have to report us if we did not stop. We used all our powers of persuasion on them, explaining how, under our training system, the student body strives to outwit the staff as part of the game and, if they joined in, the imbalance in size of our flights would probably never be noticed.

We obviously had some pretty powerful advocates for they saw the advantages of our scheme. For the remaining two months of the course only 80 per cent of both British and US cadets appeared on each morning parade and this was never detected by the staff.

We did break their Honour Code perhaps, but it did marvels for our corporate spirit. I often wondered how those US cadets got on later – they were a fine bunch. If nothing else I am sure it would have helped any who were unfortunate enough to become prisoners of war.

Air Marshal Sir Patrick Hine

In the early days of the Harrier there was no two-seat version; consequently, all training was conducted in the single-seat GR1, with verbal encouragement from an instructor on the ground, callsign Pegasus, working in a specially constructed mobile caravan. By and large the conversions to type went well, since the pilots were experienced aircrew and the pre-flight preparation was thorough. However, occasionally there was some excitement and this tale concerns one of those times.

The pilot involved had many hours on the Hunter, but was naturally new to the Harrier and all it entailed – vectored thrust, the ability to take off and land vertically, and an unusual undercarriage arrangement that utilized two of the four sets of wheels near the wing tips. The occasion was the pilot's first hover, a moment of some concern to even the most hard-bitten pilots. The aircraft was lined up on the concrete pad, the pilot ran through his checks and tested the nozzles under the watchful eye of Pegasus sitting some two hundred yards away. When all was ready the pilot, instead of moving the nozzles to the vertical position, moved them only to the 40° angle, and before Pegasus could say anything the throttle was opened and the aircraft staggered forward, tipping down alarmingly on to its nose. The pilot corrected the pitch down – but not in time to prevent the nose probe bending through about 60° – then corrected the nozzle angle and lurched unsteadily into the air. Looking most unusual in its new configuration, the aircraft then meandered around rather uncertainly over the pad, whilst the pilot recovered his composure and Pegasus offered words of advice on how to land – generally the trickier of the two operations.

Some three or four minutes later calm was restored and our hero (now, incidentally, a very experienced and respected Harrier 'mate') was in a position to land, and did so with precision and aplomb. Everyone breathed a sigh of relief and Pegasus, in a reference to the Harrier's outrigger wheels, defused the situation by calling encouragingly over the air: 'Next time we take off the training wheels.'

*

During the Falklands War there were many servicemen working in the Ministry of Defence who were frustrated and even annoyed that they could not take a greater part in the operations. One such young man, a Harrier pilot, was getting progressively more irate about his lack of impact when he received the following letter, enclosed in a very official envelope and heavily overstamped with red secrecy markings:

Dear Squadron Leader Bloggs,

You are no doubt aware of the serious situation that has arisen in the Falkland Islands and the resulting drastic repercussions that have compelled the government to take necessary action to protect the sovereignty of these Islands.

The government are urgently compiling a list of people whom we think would be of the calibre to undertake arduous, dangerous and essentially secret duties on our behalf: your name has been put forward as a suitable candidate.

There are few options open to the government but it is proposed that we infiltrate the Falkland Islands with such stealth and speed that the Argentinian invaders would be taken completely by surprise. Initially one school of thought is to disguise a group of volunteers as penguins so that they may land on the island without arousing too much suspicion. These penguins would then reconnoitre the island causing as much damage as possible by sabotaging military installations, i.e., dropping penguin eggs down gun turrets etc., and to set up road blocks by means of general gathering and strutting about as penguins are prone to do.

This is where you come in; we have studied your statistics and feel that you are the ideal size and shape for one of these penguins. It would, of course, mean that you would not be registered under the Ministry of Defence but the Ministry of Fisheries: other than this we can see no overwhelming obstacles to this venture.

Perhaps you would be kind enough to report to me as soon as possible so that you may be measured for your outfit and also change your diet as soon as possible to fish.

The letter didn't help his frustration but it did restore his sense of humour.

Air Chief Marshal
Sir Thomas Kennedy
and his Staffs at the Ministry of Defence

My predecessor left me with one piece of advice – 'Be brief.' The briefest after-dinner speech I am told was made by a senior member of the Royal and Ancient Golf Club who, on being asked to speak, got to his feet and said, 'Gentlemen, I give you whisky and water – you will be prosecuted if you make the first in private or the second in public.'

*

The captain of a bomber or reconnaissance aircraft was on a long sortie. It was a routine straight and level flight but he had a crack crew with an extremely smart and accurate navigator. All of a sudden he was instructed by the navigator to turn 90 degrees to port, which he did, and then 90 degrees to starboard. That was hotly pursued by another order to turn 90 degrees to starboard and then 90 degrees to port. He couldn't understand the reason for the sudden deviation before coming back to the original track. (One must remember that in those days navigators had long charts and a sliding chair.) The captain later discovered that a baked bean had been dropped on to the chart and his navigator, in an attempt to avoid dirtying his crisp white cuffs, had navigated the aircraft around the bean.

(*Attributed to Air Marshal Barraclough*)

★

Date: End of Second World War.
Place: Cairo – Shepherd's Hotel, top floor suite.
Event: A riotous party late at night when, after persistent knocking on the front door of the suite, the host opened it to find a monocled gentleman wearing a silk dressing gown who said, 'I am Major The Honourable Fortescue-Smythe and I live in the rooms below. Would you kindly stop making so much noise. I cannot sleep.'

Answer from host, 'Well, I'm Group Captain the Earl of Bandon, which has got you on both counts! Either go away and stop complaining, or come in and join the party!'

★

The following lines are extracts from actual confidential reports, and reflect, perhaps, the more humorous side of the personnel business.

1ST REPORTING OFFICER (RO): He has done himself a power of good over the past year and made the most of every opportunity open to him.
2ND RO: It should be noted that Fg Off. — recently married my daughter.

2ND RO: I don't know — very well, but he must be doing a commendable job, for 7/HR from the 1st RO is akin to being recommended for the Victoria Cross.

Her personal appearance varied considerably (probably due to her pregnancy).

I see a fair amount of both Squadron Leader and Mrs —. Both are well endowed. . . .

Fg Off. — would make any concentration camp commandant's life hell. Why is he practising on me?

Were he to marry – his declared intention – I am sure everything would fall into place.

He has emerged from his first year as practical a commander of men as he would from three rounds with a polar bear.

Somewhat akin to a Labrador puppy, he has the potential to make a good dog but at the moment keeps knocking the gin bottle off the table with his tail.

His duties are so varied that anyone filling this appointment starts off at a disadvantage in that he can scarcely expect to satisfy everyone. In his case he has succeeded in going one stage further – he has satisfied no one. Nevertheless, he retains his optimism – but in this he stands alone.

. . . his 'barbershop' singing activities have recently taken him with the — Barbershop Harmony Club on to the national forum 'Opportunity Knocks'. He now has the experience and the qualities to make a first-class wing commander.

This officer has pierced his promotion ceiling.

He will always give good value while actively engaged in flying duties but will not rise to great heights on the ground.

I don't think that there is much future in the service for him unless he can be posted . . . to a larger unit where he may be able to have more time off to play golf.

Provided that he can contain his weight problem he should reach at least the rank of Group Captain.

Not too much should be made of the state of his desk; better generals than he have been guilty of untidy desks.

He is an apology for an officer, scruffy, naive, lacking gumption and unable to control his financial affairs – or his dog! Hitler would have put them both down.

Comment on an officer of the supply branch:
At heart a frustrated soldier, pilot, racing driver and deep-water sailor. Frustrated, not by lack of courage, but by very poor sight.

I feel OC Eng. Wg has been hard in down-grading the rating as Oi/c Drama Club. The station is still suffering from the traumatic shock of the last pantomime (children cried during the comedy scene and my Sqn Cdrs became hysterical during the love scene – it was horrible). However, this was not directly the fault of —, but more due to the lack of talent. His drive, enthusiasm and management were quite satisfactory. His next station might, however, wish to play safe and steer clear of Aladdin.

She has recently become engaged and intends to complete her contract.

. . . his secondary duty of successfully running two large officers' mess balls.

. . . was posted to the Dental Training Establishment as a stopgap officer.

Letter sent from the Directorate of Personnel (Ground):
Once you have had time to digest this letter and the paper. . . .

He and his equally sporting wife participate actively in station social events.

He has found time to help with the Youth Club, manage a barrack block with efficiency, escort civilian visits around the station, play sport and complete a 45 mile hill walk in just under 16 hours.

Preference for next appointment: 'WRAF PRO'

He readily joins in social occasions and leaves people with a warm feeling.

Her breadth of interest has been increased by her recent marriage to a Phantom pilot.

He is a lean six footer who looks good in or out of uniform.

Specialist comment on a doctor:
As an active participant in rugby, karate and kung-fu he is unlikely to run short of patients.

1st RO on a trainee surgeon:
He has already developed the facility of handling the nursing and ancillary staff to best effect.

He certainly does not merit more than a 5 for intelligence. At best I would see his promotion ceiling as Group Captain.

He has recently got married. This has not affected his dedication on the job neither has it lessened his wide range of hobbies and interests.

She is less happy with the more physical side of life. . . .

BSC Report on a dentist:
He thoroughly enjoyed his oral work.

(MO) He is already building up a reputation in the married quarters. . . .

The post is not particularly demanding but he has expended considerable energy in persuading others to take on the work it involves, delegating upwards, downwards and sideways with great skill.

He speaks in cultured tones in a Northern Irish accent.

His wife has played a notable part in the affairs of the station.

He has a lot of irons in the fire, but my instinct tells me that the fire will have extinguished itself long before he gets round to pulling them out.

I shall miss his dreadful jokes.

Report by OC Hospital on Matron:
She's like an old radio: turn down the volume, turn up the tone and you would get a much better performance.

He is a dedicated fisherman and has the temperament that goes with most of these characters who find a night on a rain-swept beach a stimulating experience.

I have very little knowledge of this officer but if in his absence on a round-the-world clipper race he can achieve ratings of 7s and 8s for his primary duties here at —, he has got to be very good indeed.

His greatest service achievement must have been the efforts he made to evade dismissal at the appropriate points in the selection and training processes.

And finally, a couple of errors from the typewriter:

He is slightly intolerant of lesser morals. . . .

His section leader (an Italian colonel) suffered a mild hard attack.

Stars in Battledress

David Kossoff

It was early in the war. I was an aircraft draughtsman in a large outer London factory. I was also a very new home guard, on night duty in the pavilion of the sports field.

A dark night. It was my watch, midnight till two. No patrol was asked for; just to stand or sit outside on the porch.

After an hour or so I carefully put down my rifle (I think we had rifles) and walked round the back to have a leak. As I buttoned myself and turned, a huge, broad-shouldered figure rose out of the long grass! I was unarmed, rigid with terror, and a born coward.

The figure rocked back and forth on its heels. It was the plywood, painted cut-out used for target practice. To this day I dream of it.

Clive Dunn

When I joined the army in 1940 my medical report referred to the fact that I had flat feet but that they would improve with military life.

In 1947 on 'demob', the medical officer had written: 'Flat feet will improve with civilian life.' Enough said.

Sir John Mills

The summer months consisted of boredom, laced with anxiety. The *Blitzkrieg* was on; Hitler's daily bombing raids started during May. Mary (my wife) was on tour with Fay Compton in *Fumed Oak*. With the telephone system in a chaotic state (it still is), it was impossible to make contact. The fact that I was stuck out in a field near Royston guarding a goat didn't make it any easier.

Towards the end of August we were standing to, just as dawn was breaking. London had been taking a pasting; we could see by the sky that the raid was over. The bombers – what was left of them – would be streaking for home. Suddenly, an aircraft emerged from a cloud making a beeline for the coast. Although I reckoned it might be just too high to be in range, I ordered the crew to open fire. There was tremendous excitement – the first shot fired in anger. The telephone rang a few minutes later. 'HQ here. The CO wants a word with you.'

'Sergeant Mills. Did you open fire on an aircraft this morning at 06.00 hours?'

'Yes sir,' I said. 'But I'm afraid we didn't hit it.'

'Congratulations, sergeant, the aircraft was a Wellington. Report to me 09.00 hours.'

The phone was slammed down. Oh well, bang goes that commission for good, I thought. I'll be in the ranks for the duration.

From *Up in the Clouds, Gentlemen Please* (Weidenfield & Nicolson)

Sir Harry Secombe

It was 1 September 1939 and I was up to my neck in trouble. I was seventeen, a junior pay clerk, and being besieged by a howling mob of men. The small tin hut I occupied along with my senior clerk reverberated to the blows of the angry miners. The fault was entirely mine. The men were issued with numbered pay dockets which contained what they were entitled to, and when they came to collect their pay they handed in a counterfoil which was attached to the docket. The number on the counterfoils corresponded to numbered tins in which we had placed the wages. Unfortunately, I had numbered some of the dockets wrongly.

The queue outside the hut was good-humoured at first as the men, newly up from the pit and blinking in the sunlight, waited for the pay out to start. Inside the hut the two of us were all prepared for the off. Bill Williams, the chief clerk, looked proudly at the tin boxes lining the walls. Then he said, 'OK, Harry, let's go.' I removed the covering from the pigeon hole and the first grubby numbered counterfoils came through. Deftly I handed over the tins with the corresponding numbers through the hatch. I was all brisk efficiency until the shouting started, until the miners began to open their tins and discover my mistakes. It only took a few minutes for my companion to trace the trouble and point a trembling finger of accusation in my direction, unable to speak. I dabbed at my new Clark Gable moustache nervously. 'Heh – heh,' I said backing away against the wall furthest from the pigeon hole. 'The Roneo machine must have slipped.'

That was when the banging began on the side of the hut. Men who should have been drawing £30 were horrified to find 7/6d and those who had found £30 instead of 7/6d were already making for the pub.

In the middle of all the confusion, an urgent knocking began on the door and we heard the voice of Arthur Kingdom, the colliery manager. 'Secombe, come on out.' The angry voices dropped to a lynch mob-type murmuring. Bill Williams said, 'He wants you.' I cowered against the wall shaking my head from side to side. 'No, no,' I said. I had seen too many films at the Pictorium Cinema in St Thomas not to know what could happen to me out there. I'd seen Spencer Tracy cop it in *Fury*.

The knocking began again. 'Come on, Secombe. Come out.' Suddenly I became Ronald Colman as Sidney Carton in *The Tale of Two Cities* just before he mounted the steps to the guillotine. 'I'm coming,' I shouted, squaring my meagre shoulders, and with head held high I opened the door.

Arthur Kingdom faced me grimly, behind him the miners waved angry fists. 'I've just had a call from head office,' he said. 'You're in the Terriers aren't you?' I nodded. 'You've just been called up.' I seized his hand in an ecstasy of relief. 'Hooray!' I said. 'Coward!' shouted Bill Williams through the pigeon hole.

And I ran off to war, grinning like an idiot. Apart from Hitler and Krupps I must have been the only happy man that day.

Richard Todd

A cadet sentry encounters the sound of footsteps crunching on the gravel at Sandhurst one night in 1940, the sound being made by my company commander, Major Blundell-Hollingshead-Blundell returning from a bibulous evening at the staff college.

SENTRY: 'Halt! Who goes there?'
REPLY: 'Blundell-Hollingshead-Blundell.'
SENTRY: 'Advance *one*, and be recognized!'

Jim Davidson

Over the years, it has been my great pleasure to entertain the mob – British servicemen – stationed overseas in some of the most inaccessible places on earth, including the Falklands. And I have had some great laughs with all the lads; they're a terrific bunch of people who have my utmost admiration. I've also had a few hairy moments on my travels, but the most frightening experience of my life came in 1977 when I was out on active entertainment duty in Belize. I still quake when I think about it.

We were billeted in Airport Camp in Belize City itself for most of the duration, but on one occasion we were helicoptered down for a concert in Rideo Camp, an out-of-the-way post in the heart of the jungle – five miles from Punta Gorda, near to the Guatamala border. . . . So there was plenty of activity.

One night, singer Frank Layton – who was also part of the entertainment team – and I were taken into Punta Gorda by a burly Scouse sergeant. We were driven in an army issue jeep through the dense jungle!

When we arrived at the tiny bar, the sergeant seemed to be the local personality and duly introduced us to everyone present. When we left at midnight, a little worse for the drink, he told us that he had let the jeep be taken back to camp, and we must get a cab! I thought he was mad. Where do you get a cab from in the middle of the jungle?

Then it all got a bit confused. In the darkness outside there was a crowd of lads milling around the bar. I thought from the revelry that had taken place inside that they were all friends of the sergeant, and I wasn't particularly worried when he jumped on the back of one of the lads in a playful piggy-back action . . . until the rest of the crowd attacked the soldier, and started beating him up. The drink must have started to take effect on me, because in the next instant, I piled in with a rescue bid only to come face to face with a knife-wielding yob with murder in his eyes. It's amazing how quickly you sober up in a situation like that! Well . . . Frank and I did the only thing we could – *withdraw*. We ran like hell. . . .

We reached the jungle and in the first clearing we found five separate tracks leading off deeper into the undergrowth. Not knowing where on earth we were, and shaking like leaves with fear in case we were caught, we ran blindly down the nearest track. And kept on running, running, running. I was convinced we were being caught. It was killing me. Poor old Frank looked dead on his feet, but we daren't stop. In the intense heat of the night added to the sharp intake of alcohol, we both became badly dehydrated. Then my boy scout training came back to me . . . and I looked around for a pebble to suck, to bring the saliva back to my mouth. I picked up what I thought was a smooth stone and put it in my mouth. It was a dead land crab! Urgghhh!

We had been running now for over three hours, deeper and deeper into the jungle, until I suddenly spotted the distant mountain landmark that I knew would take us back to camp. We'd chosen the correct pathway after all. But that single moment of relief turned suddenly to blind terror, when we heard footsteps behind us, gaining, gaining . . . I thought: these people *never* give in.

In that moment, we threw ourselves into the undergrowth for cover and landed in a muddy pile of rotting vegetation. Phew! It stank! but we didn't worry, we had other things on our mind, and I was convinced that my pounding heart would crash straight through my chest in a few minutes. I was rigid with fear as the footsteps neared . . . and suddenly stopped.

Like some demented idiot, I called out. 'Sarge, is that you? Sarge?' And in a second the footsteps sped off again at great pace.

We waited . . . and waited.

When we realized it was safe to come out of our jungle hideaway, we continued our journey back to camp and eventually we found our way home, half dead with exhaustion and smelling like a waste disposal unit. But we made it.

In the guardroom later, we came face to face with the footsteps in the shape of a Gurkha sergeant. He had been out on an exercise, making his way back to camp, when he suddenly heard the jungle talking to him . . . calling his name . . . and there was nobody there. He didn't stop to investigate, but ran the quickest two miles back to camp ever recorded!

We didn't let on.

Donald Sinden

After Dunkirk the whole of the south coast was barricaded and only residents were allowed within fifteen miles of the coast. Gun emplacements had been dotted along the shore. We heard at first hand the story of General Montgomery coming down to inspect the defences and asking a young subaltern if there were any problems: 'Yes, sir,' he said pointing to his map. 'There are Howitzers here and here with a range of X yards, twenty-five pounders here and here with a range of Y yards, and anti-tank guns here and here with a range of Z yards – this leaves a stretch of coast twenty yards long quite undefended. Suppose the Germans were to land there! – what should we do?'

'Count them as they come ashore, ring me up, tell me how many and I'll tell you what to do,' replied Monty.

We took our plays to these gun emplacements and to ack-ack sites on the Sussex Downs. Never since have I known such enthusiastic reception or such audience participation. We were at one with them: from the hilarious moment in *Private Lives* when, shortly after Elyot has uttered the delightful Coward line 'Don't quibble, Sybil', he handed her a cocktail and as she raised it to her lips a voice from the audience shouted, 'Don't dribble, Sybil', to the uncanny experience we had when playing Terence Rattigan's *French Without Tears* to an RAF audience.

The performance was going splendidly and the audience were on their toes, responding to every nuance, when suddenly halfway through the second act the laughter ceased. Silence. . . . What had happened? We cast questioning looks at each other. We continued the dialogue haltingly . . . and then . . . stopped. We became aware of a concerted murmur . . . Wrrr . . . Trrr . . . Thrrr . . . Frrr.

Unbeknown to us a squadron had set out from that RAF station during the afternoon. Now they were returning and the entire audience was counting them in as their ears picked up the drone of the engines . . . Five . . . Six . . . Seven . . . Thank God – on that occasion – they all returned. As the last was heard a cheer went up. We had all been facing each other for – what? – thirty minutes? The audience had never ceased looking in our direction, but were oblivious of our presence. Now we could breathe again and we continued with the scene to much laughter – laughter tinged with a certain hysteria – laughter of a quality I will probably never hear again.

*

A friend of mine in the regular army had to deliver a highly important message to headquarters in the middle of the night. Sitting in the back seat of a staff car, he was being driven at top speed through the Sussex lanes when a waving red light from a home guard post could be seen ahead. The driver started to slow down, but was ordered to drive straight through. Muffled figures leaped out of the way. Fifty yards further on a bullet shattered the rear window. Seconds later a second shot missed my friend by inches and buried itself in the backside of the driver. The car swerved to a standstill. Up came an elderly and

142

panting home guard waving a smoking Lee-Enfield rifle and shouting, 'It's a good job you did stop – I wouldn't have fired the third shot in the air!'

From *A Touch of the Memoirs* (Hodder & Stoughton)

Frankie Howerd

I remember going into drag for one concert, dressed as an ATS girl. This wasn't the modern transvestite concept of looking glamorously feminine – my version was the traditional pantomime travesty of femininity. Absurdly large balloons, not a padded bra, served as breasts, while my make-up was a grotesque mouth lipsticked to cover half my lower face, and my wig was made of straw. I sang a comic song in the role of an old ATS scrubber. Nothing dirty, however – I was too innocent for such material, as you shall see.

Anyway, in the middle of this song an alert sounded. The audience stampeded for the exit, and I rushed backstage. I had time to change into my own uniform, but not to remove my make-up. So there I was on parade with rifle and pack – and this face!

A young subaltern came to inspect the ranks. He arrived at where I was standing . . . moved on . . . stopped . . . shook his head as though not believing what he had seen – and turned. I tried to stand rigidly to attention, but body and rifle trembled.

The officer stared at me, but I kept my eyes focused on the far side of the parade ground. After some hours of silence on both sides (or was it seconds?) the officer permitted himself a discreet question mark of a cough.

'C-concert party, sir,' I explained, my eyes still fixed straight ahead. 'The alert went in the m-middle of the

143

c-concert party.' The situation was in no way helped by panic strangling my voice into a squeaky falsetto.

'Concert party. . . Er yes. . . Mmmm . . . Concert party . . . jolly good. . . . ' He moved along the line, but from the corner of my eye I could see him turn his head, turn it away again, shake it – slowly this time, as though debating whether the sight he had just seen was a matter for the military police or the medical officer.

★

Now I know this sounds like something out of one of my acts, but it's absolutely true: I was an interpreter! Worse was to come. . . .

Sergeant F. Howerd was posted to Brussels, seconded to the military government. I asked, with some trepidation, 'Who are we governing?' and they said, 'The Germans soon, because we're winning the war,' and I said, 'That's one blessing, anyway.'

And I was sent off to a village with a major who couldn't speak a word of French to discover if there were any expectant mothers there: they'd get priority when food was distributed. 'It's jolly simple,' said the major. 'All you have to do is tell them we want to know of any women who are pregnant.'

I went to rehearse. . . .

I didn't know the French for pregnant, but I reckoned I could make do with, 'We'd like to know if any woman is going to have a baby.'

So I worked out, 'We is: *nous* . . . We would like is: *nous voulons* . . . To know is: *savoir* . . . If is: *si* . . . Any woman . . . I don't know about "any", but woman is: *une femme* . . . Is going is: *allons* . . . To have is: *avoir*, and a child is: *enfant* . . . So there we are: *Nous voulons savoir si une femme allons avoir un enfant.*'

After some practice, I decided to chance my arm and walk around the village asking this, adding a few oo-la-lahs and a touch of the hooded-eyed, purse-lipped Charles Boyer's to give it an authentic Gallic flay-veur.

The first woman I tried it on looked at me blankly; the second bleakly. The third frowned and sidled away. The fourth screamed and fled – to return with an enormous brute of a man with vast biceps that seemed to positively throb. Encouraged by his presence, other men and women arrived – and the fact that many were carrying cudgels, pitchforks and shotguns I put down to their patriotic fervour: they were ready to fight to the death should the Germans counterattack.

The man with the muscles machine-gunned a burst of French at me. I attempted what was meant to be a noncommital shrug, then repeated my carefully rehearsed statement in French.

A murmur, a muttering, a gesticulation with cudgels, pitchforks and shotguns – and a slow, shuffling advance. It dawned on my tiny mind that I wasn't going down all that well, so I took a step backwards. . . . They took two steps forwards. . . . Even a mathematical novice will realize that in this backwards-forwards proportion it wasn't long before Mr Universe (Belgian branch) was breathing garlic up my nostrils.

I cocked my rifle – then realized I'd left it back at the hotel.

With a shrill howl I skidded round on my heel – and fled.

It transpired that something had gone a trifle wrong in the translation: instead of saying that we wanted to know whether any woman was having a baby, I'd asked if any woman wanted to have a baby!

The major and I hastened from the village – and got lost in a sudden fog.

Alex Gordon

The famed motto of the postal service was never more in evidence than in 1942 when, as a youngster of nineteen, I was in the RASC attached to the 11 Armoured Division stationed in Newmarket prior to going overseas. The Second World War had interrupted my activities as head of the British Gene Autrey Fan Club, honouring the original Singing Cowboy of movies and records and issuing a quarterly magazine, the *Westerner*, for five thousand club members.

A final issue explaining cessation of the magazine's publication until war's end was due, but army postal censors refused to consider my plea to mail five thousand copies with the admonition that they had neither the time nor manpower to read that number. In vain I tried to reason with the logical thought that only one copy need be read, the others being identical printing, but no such explanation was accepted.

'Not snow, nor rain, nor heat, nor gloom of night stays these couriers from the swift completion of their appointed rounds' reads the motto of the postal service, and I felt strongly that this applied in the present situation. Thus a speedy meeting on compassionate grounds with the division chaplain, who moved me through channels from second lieutenant to captain, thence major, lieutenant-colonel, and finally, my knees quaking, face to face with the major general in charge of the entire shebang.

He understood perfectly – and assigned two staff sergeants to help me stuff the envelopes, stamp them and get them out to the anxious club members all over the world.

No wonder we won the war.

Spike Milligan

Lugging a suitcase tied with traditional knotted string, I made my way to Headquarters 56th Heavy Regiment Royal Artillery. Using sign language they redirected me to D Battery. They were stationed in a building called Worthingholm, an evacuated girls' school in Hastings Road. As I entered the drive, a thing of singular military ugliness took my eye. It was Battery Sergeant Major 'Jumbo' Day. His hair was so shorn his neck seemed to go straight up the back of his hat, and his face was suffused red by years of drinking his way to promotion. 'Oi! Where yew goin'? It ain't a girls' school no more.'

'Isn't it? Never mind, I'll join the regiment instead,' I said.

He screwed up his eyes. 'You're not Milligan, are yew?'

'Actually I am.'

A beam of sadistic pleasure spread over his face.

'We've been waiting for yew!' he said, pushing me ahead of him with his stick. He drove me into what was D Battery Office. The walls once white were now thrice grey. From a peeling ceiling hung a forty watt bulb that when lit made the room darker. A Janker wallah was giving the bare floor a stew-coloured hue by slopping a mop around, rearranging the dirt. On the wall was a calendar with a naked tart advertising cigarettes. Below it was a newspaper cut-out of Neville Chamberlain grinning upwards. Fronting the fireplace was a trestle table covered with a merry grey blanket. A pile of OHMS letters, all addressed to me, was tucked in the corner of the blotter. In the lid of a cardboard shoe-box was a collection of rubber bands, paper-clips, sealing wax, string and a lead weight. My pulses raced! Here was the heart of a great fighting machine. Seated behind this mighty war organ was a middle-aged, pink, puffy-faced man in his early fifties wearing a uniform in its late seventies. Parts that had frayed had been trimmed with leather; these included cuffs, elbows, pockets, gaiters and all trailing edges; for this reason he was known as

'Leather Suitcase'. His maiden name was Major Startling-Grope. 'This is Gunner Milligan, sir,' said the BSM. When they'd both finished laughing, the major spoke.

'Whair hev yew been, and whai are yew wearing civilian clothes?'

'They wouldn't let me on the train naked, sir.'

'I mean, whai aren't you in uniform?'

'Silence when you speak to an officer,' said BSM.

The major, who was fiddling with a rubber band, slid it over his finger.

'Does this mean we're engaged, sir?'

'Silence!' said BSM.

'I suppose,' said Suitcase, 'you know you are three months late arriving?'

'I'll make up for it, sir, I'll fight nights as well!' All these attempts at friendly humour fell on stony ground. I was marched to a bare room by a bombardier. He pointed to a floor board.

'You're trying to tell me something,' I said.

'Your bed, right?'

'Right.'

'Right, bombardier!'

'I'm a bombardier already?'

'Oh, cheeky bastard, eh? Got the very job for yew.'

He gave me a scrubbing brush with two bristles, showed me a three-acre cook-house floor and pointed down; he was still trying to tell me something. Leering over all this was the dwarf-like battery cook, Bombardier Nash, who looked like Quasimodo with the hump reversed. He was doing things to sausages. Three hours' scrubbing, and the knees in my trousers went through. To make matters worse there were no uniforms in the 'Q' stores. I cut a racy figure on guard, dark blue trousers gone at the knee, powder blue double-breasted chalk-stripe jacket, lemon shirt and white tie, all set off with steel helmet, boots and gaiters. It wasn't easy.

'Halt! Who goes there?' I'd challenge. When they saw me the answer was, 'Piss off.' I had to be taken off guard duties. In time I got a uniform. It made no difference.

'Halt, who goes there?'

'Piss Off.'

Words can't describe the wretched appearance of a soldier in a new battle-dress. Size had nothing to do with it. You wore what you got. Some soldiers never left barracks for fear of being seen. Others spent most of their time hiding behind trees. The garments were impregnated with an anti-gas agent that reeked like dead camels, and a water-proofing chemical that gave you false pregnancy and nausea. The smell of 500 newly kitted rookies could only be likened to an open Hindu sewerage works on a hot summer night by Delius. To try and 'cure' my BD I salted it and hung it outside in thunderstorms, I took it for walks, I hit it, in desperation, I sprayed it with eau de Cologne, it made little difference, except once a sailor followed me home. Overcoats were a huge, shapeless dead loss. If you wanted alterations, you took it to a garage. But the most difficult part of army life was the 0600 hours awakening. In films this was done by a smart bugler who, silhouetted against the dawn with the Union Jack flying, blew reveille. Not so our 'Badgey',* who stayed in bed, pushed the door open with his foot, blew reveille, then went back to sleep.

From *Adolf Hitler: My Part in his Downfall* (Michael Joseph)

*Badgey: bugler

Norman Wisdom

Being with the British Army in India, as a band boy and trumpeter with the Tenth Royal Hussars just before the war, was, and probably still is, the happiest and most exciting time of my life.

In the first place, I had joined in order to have regular food and somewhere to sleep, but I soon found that sport, self-discipline, camaraderie and humour were equally, if not more, acceptable. Without a shadow of a doubt the army was totally responsible for the fortunate success that I had in later life.

Show business is a tough business. You need to have luck, plus talent, and then that little bit of disarming cocky cheekiness that can help you in the right direction. This short narrative leads to an incident which occurred on parade one morning, as the officer walked along to inspect us.

At this time I was nearly sixteen and very smart. The officer stopped in front of me, looked me up and down with some approval, and then, looking at my face upon which a proud little growth of fluff was beginning to sprout, he said, with a smile, 'Wisdom, you're beginning to need a shave.' It was completely taboo to answer an officer back, but I found it irresistible. 'I'm beginning to grow a moustache, sir,' I said. He became a little more stern, and wiping his hand all round my face and neck to demonstrate the growth, he said, 'But, Wisdom, you don't grow a moustache all round here.' I didn't intend to answer but somehow I did. 'No sir, but I haven't trimmed it yet!'

There were screams of laughter from the whole parade, which included the inspecting officer, who, whilst still laughing, retorted, 'Very funny, Wisdom! See me in the office.'

I did just that and I got seven days defaulters, or 'jankers', as it was called then.

I may also mention that the officer was the entertainments officer and from then on I was in the concert pary.

Charlie Chester

As sergeant-in-charge of one of the Stars in Battledress units, we entertained serving soldiers practically everywhere. Front line, desert, Nissen huts, garrison theatres . . . mud fields . . . NAAFI counters, and even lorry tailboards.

One of the most disconcerting places was underground in an ammunition dump where they had platforms and trains hauling the ammunition to and fro.

The troops were stationed on one platform, and we had to do our show to them from the opposite platform.

This was fine except that for a comic there is nothing worse than to begin a routine of patter, or a story . . . only to have a long train chugging past between you and the audience . . . Did you hear the one about the fella . . . diddley bom . . . diddley bom . . . diddley bom . . . who went to the doctor . . . diddley bom . . . diddley bom . . . it wasn't easy!

The worst I ever encountered, and it happened to me twice, was when we were sent to an outlandish place to entertain the troops somewhere in England. We started to a great cheer; the knockout sketches went well, the musical acts went like a bomb, the singers did well, but me as top of the bill – I died on my feet with my comedy routines of patter.

At the end of the show I said to the sergeant major, 'I wonder why they didn't like me?' He said, 'Oh they liked you all right, they just didn't understand you – this is the *Polish* brigade.'

*

I remember at Honiton in Devon entertaining the ATS girls – and what a marvellous audience they were. My saucy patter got roars but when I went on as a Hula girl with long black hair and a sarong – with saucepan lids on elastic for a bra – they went hysterical, and when Eddie Leroy bounded on as a caveman in tights with long red hairs on them, plus a wild-looking wig and wearing a leopard skin, they fell about. We proceeded to do the famous bubble dance with a large balloon (which is a funny routine anyway) and in one of the quieter moments one poor girl couldn't stop and we suddenly heard water trickling – this poor lass was so uncontrollable with laughter she had wet herself. It was a moment I shall never forget. Despite the embarrassment she was still laughing when they carried her out on a stretcher.

★

Every touring show will know the value of 'crossovers' – quick little interruptions which get an immediate laugh. The troops love these simple little things like a man walking across the stage with a stick, hitting a prop leg of ham. The straight man says, 'What are you doing?' and the first man says, 'I'm flogging the rations.' A cert laugh is quickly followed by another in quickfire sessions. However, in the desert one is likely to suffer what is known as gippy tummy, and one can also feel sick – the conditions make no excuses for entertainers.

Buddy Graham (of the Graham Brothers, a palladium hokum act) and I were doing the crossovers while Peter Forbes held centre stage. The only trouble was that I was feeling sick as a dog – and poor Buddy had trouble the other end. To facilitate matters we had a large pioneer bucket in the wings each side of the stage, and as we crossed over to do our funnies I was sick in one – and he obliged the other end. Then we crossed over and did a repeat performance. It's not always easy in show business!

Hughie Green

In 1944, under 'lend lease' agreement, the Russians were given ninety flying boats by the Americans. Soviet navy pilots were dispatched via Siberia and Alaska to pick up the giant Catalina boats and be trained in the sleepy old east-coast town of Elizabeth City, North Carolina, by the US Navy. From this magnolia blossom paradise, in summer, when the lakes of Canada and Newfoundland were ice free, our vodka-drinking allies flew them home to Murmansk via Gander and Reykjavik, Iceland. At the time of this event I was an RCAF flight-lieutenant attached to RAF Ferry Command, Montreal. With other Commonwealth-trained flying boat pilot navigators, I was drawn into this allied act of friendship when the Americans decided training our mutual friends was 'enough'. 'Let the Limeys ferry them home to Russia,' was their unselfish cry. The 'honour' sold to us in Montreal by those we saluted, and who were not coming with us, we quickly learned was a hollow one, for arriving in Elizabeth City it was made quite plain that our transatlantic flying companions were as ill-equipped to speak English as we were to pass the time of day in Russian.

Having spent many hours on coastal command Cats patrolling the chilling and awesome wastes of the North Atlantic out of bases in Nova Scotia, I was aware of the dangers that could be encountered flying across one of the world's most forbidding oceans with seven men who'd never had the experience before and none of whom could speak English. For communication we had a simple phrase book compiled by an idiot who had supplied us with such cosy expressions as, 'Is your mother well?', 'How's your father?', 'Can I have a date with your sister?' (a vain hope), instead of more practical requests such as 'Mind the mountain', 'Watch your bloody air speed' or, worst of all, 'We're lost'. As the Russians were actually to be at the controls, and we were only there to take over in an 'emergency', on our first night in Elizabeth City my fellow pilots and I quickly repaired to the bar and enquired from their American instructors as to the Russian students' prowess when it came to flying boats. These, to put it mildly, frantic enquiries were greeted with wry smiles and the ominous words, 'Have a drink, pal.'

In the cold wee hours of the following morning, the blood drained from my face and the face of my engineer – the only other English-speaking crew companion I had aboard – when the Russian skipper abandoned two take-offs and only managed to drag the huge water bird into the air on the third attempt. We travelled in groups of four – despite begging them not to try and fly the ungainly boats in formation all those Atlantic bad-weather miles, they were determined to do so. This produced hair-raising results; one moment you could shake hands with the crew in the next boat and two minutes later you needed a pair of binoculars to see them. Seniority was much respected in the soviet navy, and, as I flew with the number two man, protocol demanded we had to land just after and right behind the leader, usually a colonel. Yes, they had army ranks for naval flyers. (On our first spine-chilling trip, en route to Gander Lake, the weather closed Gander and we were obliged to divert to the American station at Argentia, site of Churchill's and President Roosevelt's much-publicized wartime meeting. Situated on the rocky southeastern tip of usually fog-bound 'Newfie', as a quickly built wartime base, it was well endowed with deep water naval facilities, as well as runways and a vast well-sheltered water alighting area for flying boats.)

After our one thousand miles of nerve-wracking formation flying from Elizabeth City, I was glad to see it, and, contemplating the ability of my Russian captain to put us safely back on the water after his three tries at getting us off, I managed with lots of grunts and sign language to remove the co-pilot from his seat, and was now sitting beside the captain, with a set of dual controls comfortingly in front of me. After much shouting in

Russian, with a reverberating klunk the huge retracting wing-tip floats fell into position as the giant water bird slowly wheeled round on to final approach. Dead ahead and slightly below was the lead boat with the colonel at the controls. Despite the fact there was miles of water on either side to land on, sticking to protocol my captain jockeyed our boat in descent and stayed right behind the leader. Two white plumes of spray and a sudden wake on the landing area surface told me the colonel was safely down.

Our engines screamed as the captain of my boat put the propellors into high pitch. Apprehensive, I judged we'd land just behind the leader. The water came up fast. My bloke cut the power off and pulled the nose up for the touch down. 'Too high, too high,' I yelled uselessly in English, as we kissed the surface and, like a stone you skim on water, bounced back into the air and right over the lead boat which was now safely taxiing on the water. Realizing it was underneath us and we were liable to stall on top of it, for a split second I watched my petrified Russian sitting in the captain's seat doing nothing. Grabbing the controls I rammed forward the throttles and with full power staggered over the colonel's Catalina to splash down in the water ahead of him. Protocol had been broken, but thank God nothing else had.

An hour after our somewhat unorthodox arrival at Argentia the admiral bought me a drink. 'You know, Green,' he said, 'I've been around flying boats for twenty years of my life, but that's the first time I ever saw one playing leap frog.'

On the Home Front

Ronnie Barker

A friend of mine, home on leave from the army, took his wife on a shopping trip to London. While his wife popped into Boots, the chemist, in Piccadilly, he stood outside, drinking in the sights and sounds of the bustling thoroughfare.

He was approached by a most attractive lady of the streets, who sidled up to him and purred in his ear, 'Hello soldier boy – like a good time?' exhibiting about three and a half pounds of cleavage as she did so. By way of making polite conversation he enquired how much. 'Two pound, dearie,' said the demi-mondaine, bouncing her heavenly twins once again in his direction.

'What each, or the pair?' he replied in jocular fashion.

'Come on, I like the look of you,' she continued, ignoring his prevarication. 'Two pounds, darling.'

'I'm not paying all that,' said my friend, and offered her thirty shillings. 'Thirty bob?' she said scornfully, 'You'll be lucky, sonny Jim. You won't get much for that round here,' and wiggled her way disdainfully on her stiletto heels, heading for Soho.

An hour later, when he and his wife were walking arm-in-arm down Lisle Street on their way to a little Italian restaurant for lunch, there, in a doorway, stood the same pretty tart. Looking his wife up and down disdainfully, she called across the street, 'There you are – I told you you wouldn't get much for thirty bob.'

HRH Prince Andrew

Two cannibals, father and son, were walking through the jungle when they spied through the trees a fair maiden. The son, not well up on the facts of life, said, 'Look at her, Father, why don't we take her home and eat her for dinner?'

His father replied, 'I have a better idea – we'll take her home and eat your mother.'

David Penhaligon
Member of Parliament

I was born on 6 June 1944 – D-Day – and I have always regarded as my first piece of political luck the failure of my mother's efforts to have me christened Montgomery. As I am sure you can appreciate, Penhaligon represents some difficulties when designing election posters but Montgomery Penhaligon would be beyond the ingenuity of even Saatchi and Saatchi!

The Honourable
Charles Morrison
Member of Parliament

Whilst making his annual state of the nation speech, the leader of a newly developing country said, 'Last year our country was on the edge of a precipice. This year we shall take a great leap forward.'

Colonel the Right Honourable
Sir Edward du Cann
Member of Parliament

The trouble with political jokes is that some of them get elected.

Lieutenant-General
M. C. L. Wilkins
Commandant General Royal Marines

A couple who had been married for fifty years decided to test the 'life after death' theory. They decided that whoever died first the other partner would try, for one year, to get through. A couple of years later the husband died and every week for a year the wife went to a medium to try to get through to her husband. However, she had no success with this venture until the last week before the year was up.

She began by asking her husband what life was like. 'Well,' he replied, 'I am having an absolutely marvellous time here. I can do exactly as I please. If I want to have a lie-in then I can, and when I get up I can have exactly what I want for breakfast. There is always plenty of fresh fruit and veg. that I can just go and pick whenever I want. If I fancy a little bit during the morning I can choose whoever I want, and then after lunch (again of fresh fruit and veg. that I pick) I have a little sleep. In the afternoons and evenings I can do just as I like, and if I feel like another little bit followed by a sleep that is just what I do. Life couldn't be better.'

'Good grief,' said his wife, 'I didn't know Heaven was like that.'

'Heaven?' said the husband, 'I'm not in heaven – I'm a rabbit on Salisbury Plain!'

Air Marshal Sir Michael Knight

A very senior officer was appointed governor of one of the Channel Islands – in which capacity he was expected to be something of an instant authority on a certain breed of cattle. Soon after taking up his appointment, he was being driven in his open-topped limousine to attend the first of many cattle shows, and as his cavalcade approached the official marquee, he heard the following over the public address system.

> Now ladies and gentlemen, we come to the Open Class for Prize Old Pedigree Bulls – and, at this point, I'd ask you all to rise to greet His Excellency the Governor.

*

A very famous wartime pilot was given to the occasional touch of acerbity in his comments. During a lull in conversation at a rather grand civic dinner in Gloucestershire, he delivered himself of the firm opinion that the only good things ever to come out of Wales were rugby players and prostitutes. A high civic dignitary was outraged. 'I'll have you know, sir, that my own wife is Welsh!'

'How interesting,' replied our imperturbable hero, 'What position does she play?'

Admiral Sir Peter Herbert
Vice-Chief of the Defence Staff

A friend of mine received the following letter from his daughter at school. It goes:

Dear Darling Mummy & Daddy,
    I hope you are well. It is raining here. I hope Spot (the dog) has found his ball and Whiskers (the cat) is eating properly.
    The other day something really 'wow' happened. We had a fire in our dormy. It started at the fire escape and cut us all off. I thought I was going to die. Smoke was everywhere. Suddenly there was a crack at the window by my bed and a ladder appeared; then a helmet; then a face. Golly, Mummy, please believe me, but I knew at once I was in love.
    As you will have seen from the postmark I am now in Southend living with Bert. We live in a caravan and it's a bit damp. Bert is now unemployed and we have no money. The worst thing is – I think I'm pregnant.

Lots & lots of love – and hopes for some money.
Cynthia.

PS None of the above is true but I have failed my 'O' levels and felt that you ought to get things in perspective and get your priorities right.

Paddy Ashdown
Member of Parliament

Amongst a rather limited range of attributes, I am able to speak Chinese, having studied the language and the culture for two and a half years. I don't know quite how it happened but I got myself on to the Women's Institute Speaking Circuit about four or five years ago, speaking on the subject of China. I was invited on one summer's evening to go to a local village Women's Institute to give my talk. I remember noticing as I entered the hall a rather splendid collection of jugs, vases, teacups, etc., sitting on a table at the back, and thinking to myself that tea was clearly going to be served in a rather more miscellaneous but nevertheless grander collection of receptacles than was normally the case. As it happened on my arrival, the Women's Institute were discussing their previous National Annual General Meeting in the Albert Hall. I remember thinking to myself, as they discussed some very important national issues, that they did a rather better job of debating the key issues of our day then we do in the House of Commons!

However, as soon as the discussion was finished I was introduced and my talk on China was announced with flourish. I recall quite clearly noticing the quizzical look which passed across the faces of my audience as I started to explain Chinese history, the thoughts of Mao Tse-Tung, Chinese art, language, etc. I am very nervous when I speak, however, and so am not very able to respond to the mood of my audience, preferring instead to ignore it. This I did.

It came as a surprise, therefore, when at the end of my talk I was profusely thanked by the chairwoman of the Women's Institute who said, 'Mr Ashdown, we found your talk most interesting, but it was not at all what we expected. Actually we thought you were going to talk about Wedgwood and Spode, that was why we all brought our bits of china along for you to see!'

Legion Lines

Major Tony Morgan
Secretary of The Poppy Appeal

During 1984 we had a poster campaign for the Poppy Appeal – the idea being to encourage all our local honorary organizers to display, or have displayed, as many posters as possible in their local area. This campaign was in general very successful, and in one district of London it was noticed that the local vicar must have thought a similar campaign might increase the size of his congregation.

Almost overnight the churchyard was covered in posters with the slogan, 'If you're tired of sin, step in'.

We later heard that the vicar was very upset when he noticed someone had written in large letters under the most prominent poster, 'If you're not, phone Piccadilly 3075.'

General Sir Patrick Howard-Dobson
National President, The Royal British Legion

A gallant and distinguished brigadier retired and took over as secretary of an equally distinguished golf club not a thousand miles from Windsor. Soon after taking over he was walking round the course one evening and found to his amazement a couple putting a bunker to a use for which it was not designed. 'I say,' he said, 'you can't do that here!'

'Why?' said the young man, pausing in his work.

'Well,' said the brigadier, unaccustomed to having his orders questioned, 'you're not members, are you?'

The Right Honourable
Nicholas Winterton
Member of Parliament

I recall that a member of the British Legion, who worked as a sorter in the local post office, was surprised to come across a letter addressed in a childish hand to 'Dear God-in-Heaven'. He opened it, not quite knowing what else to do with it, and read: 'Dear God-in-Heaven, I am only seven, and my mother is a widow-woman. She is very poor, and we haven't much to eat. Could you please send us £5.'

The sorter, being a decent sort, took the letter along to the Legion that night. The members had a whip-round, and made up a sum of £3.50. They deputed one of their number to take it along to the address given in the letter. Two days later, another letter, addressed to 'Dear God-in-Heaven', arrived at the post office. The sorter opened it. It read: 'Dear God-in-Heaven. Thank you very much for sending Mum the money. But could you please bring it yourself next time. The British Legion chap you sent round with it kept £1.50 for himself.'

E. E. Gardner
Secretary, Brimington Branch, The Royal British Legion

One morning, in the spring of 1943, seven young men were walking along a country road in Yorkshire. It was a lovely day, and peaceful; in fact the country was in the middle of the 'phoney war', when our armies were outwardly non-operational but the civilian forces were being urged to dig more coal, make more bombs, grow more food.

These seven young men, airmen, were walking back to their

billets which, because of the dispersal policy, were about two miles from an airfield.

As they went slowly along, a farmer with a tractor-drawn trailer sped past them. With one voice they called for a lift, and he stopped some forty yards in front. Thinking perhaps that they should break into a run – and didn't – he shouted, 'Come on, don't you know there's a war on?'

He wasn't to know until the dinner-time news on the radio that the RAF had bombed a target deep in Germany last night, and that these lads were the crew of a Halifax bomber. They knew there was a war on, they had just left it!

Ian Cannell
Former Member, National Executive Council,
The Royal British Legion

As a trainee radar operator I was stationed at RAF Compton Bassett – the sprawling No. 3 Radio School in the otherwise beautiful county of Wiltshire.

Part of the daily routine was a parade outside squadron headquarters, for reasons that remain obscure. The men were under the lugubrious Sergeant Mahoney – a man of long service and well accustomed to obeying his superiors' orders without question.

The squadron commander appeared with the brisk manner that seems to be kept for such occasions. 'Now look here, sergeant,' he began, 'today is Wednesday and I want to see 100 per cent sports parade this afternoon!'

Sergeant Mahoney began to look distinctly uncomfortable, shifting nervously from one foot to the other.

'But, sir!' he finally blurted out, 'Sure it's not possible!'

'Why ever not?' demanded the officer.

'Well, sir – you see, sir, there's only 96 men in the squadron!'

*

Outside the station guardroom stood the customary flagpole. One morning a provost sergeant, apparently sober, was seen trying desperately to climb up the pole, holding the end of a measuring tape in his teeth. At the bottom of the pole another provost sergeant held the other end of the tape.

Peter Holland
Area Organizer, Northwest Area, The Royal British Legion

As an inexperienced airman fresh out of the RAF Apprentice Training School I was posted to assist in the final closure of the RAF Group Headquarters at Martlesham Heath, Suffolk, in December 1960. Discipline was the order of the day at that time, and true to form I had been trained to do as told and not to ask impertinent questions such as 'Why?'

The second Tuesday of that month was a particularly cold and unpleasant day. A bitterly cold northeasterly wind swept the unit, interspersed with freezing rain and sleet. I was on an outside working party with little to do, and the last thing my corporal wanted (he was in his last month of National Service) was an energetic, bubbly, enthusiastic *regular* who actually asked for work.

Finally, in what I now realize was exasperation, he pointed across the grass-strip airfield to a small wooden hut. 'Burn that down if you are cold and want something to do,' he ordered me, before retiring to his warm office.

What a blaze! I must confess that even I was staggered at the height of the flames. Such responsibility, I mused, for one so young. How well I carried out my task and with such relish. I even had visions of early promotion!

Unfortunately, I failed to notice the 10,000 loo rolls stored in the hut. At the subsequent unit inquiry my corporal was severely reprimanded for his actions. I, of course, was cleared of all blame – I was carrying out orders.

After the inquiry my flight commander whispered in my ear, 'Well done, you can sleep peacefully at night in the certain knowledge that you have saved at least 10,000 bums from the lacerations of "Government Issue".'

*

As a young airman now two years out of training school there was little more, I thought, that life could teach me. I was living life to the full, working hard and playing hard.

I was particularly grateful to the RAF for supplying its own brand of entertainment in the form of the WRAF. How those pleasant young ladies were to further my career!

It was the third time I was caught out of bounds in the WRAF block that I was marched before my flight commander. 'There's no room in this man's air force for this kind of behaviour,' he sternly admonished me, 'Buck up or get out.' The following Monday I was promoted to the rank of corporal and posted for a most lucrative tour in Germany.

I would like to take this opportunity of recording my eternal thanks to the WRAF for bringing my name to attention and furthering my career so successfully.

Robert Scaife
National Vice-chairman, The Royal British Legion

In 1957, during my National Service days in the Royal Air Force, the time came round for the AOC's Annual Inspection. As was the practice on such occasions, coal was made blacker, grass was made greener and pebbles made whiter. A practical example of 'if it moves salute it, if it doesn't paint it'.

My place of employment was a small workshop within the barrack stores wherein I carried out repairs to various pieces of furniture and certain wooden equipment. The instruction given to me was to make the workshop spotless for the expected visit. Order given and obeyed.

The big day arrived. Airmen and airwomen were at their places of work and, in answer to a bugle call, fell-in outside their respective office or workshop. Flashes of gold braid in front of one's eyes signified that you had gained the attention of the AOC himself. Quickfire questions received short answers given in awe. The visiting party moved into my small workshop and heads were nodded in acknowledgement of its spotless condition. The AOC looked me in the eye and said, 'And what have you been doing today, airman?' An equally straightforward look from the airman with an honest response of 'Cleaning up for your inspection, sir.'

Later that same day the Squadron Leader IC Stores suffered a heart attack. Thankfully he recovered.

*

Comedy in films is often manufactured, but some events must undoubtedly be taken from real life. In one of the *Doctor* films starring Dirk Bogarde and James Robertson Justice, there was the well-known occasion when the young trainee doctor was asked by the senior surgeon as to what was the bleeding time. The quick response was ten past nine.

In 1956, on a parade at a certain Royal Air Force station in Wiltshire, the marching of a particular flight was ragged to say the least. The officer in charge, in order to present something passable, instructed a sergeant to 'call out the time'. The sergeant followed instructions but created utter chaos when from his lips came the words, 'Ten past nine, sir.'

*

Since leaving the Royal Air Force in 1958 I have often wondered as to whether that branch of the armed forces possessed a secret weapon which would have made victory a certainty in any conflict. The reason for my puzzlement was at the time, and still is, a particular item which appeared on Station Routine Orders during early 1957. The Station Routine Order read as follows:

Blankets will be aired on a Saturday morning.
If it is raining on a Saturday morning, blankets will be aired on a Friday evening.

It makes you wonder, doesn't it?

Major Bob Tomlins
General Secretary, The Royal British Legion

A raw wet winter's day in 1942. Snow in the leaden sky of Essex and the ground a sodden morass churned over by the passage of countless feet in heavy army boots.

Five of us left, out of our infantry section. The rest had dropped out one by one over the past mile – dear God, was it only a mile! – on an assault course designed by a madman for the torture of innocents. Ropes too slippery to be climbed; tarzan swings over slime-filled pits, which looked as though they would reach to the further bank but never did; barbed wire that must not be cut ('Expensive to replace, sonny!') so could only be crossed if a lunatic fell on it like a doormat while the rest trod him underfoot; deadweight ammunition boxes to be toted; packs seemingly filled with lead ingots; and what felt like deep-sea divers' boots at the ends of our legs.

Exhaustion, physical and mental, was close.

But three of the surviving five had more at stake than the rest. We wore the white epaulette flashes and lance-corporal stripes which branded us potential officers. The hawk-like eyes of every NCO for miles around seemed to be searching for signs of our weakness.

Only the wall, and the river ahead, then the firing range, and merciful relief.

Oh, that wall! Impossibly high it seemed as we staggered towards it, rifles at the trail. Tim ahead, then myself, then Mike and the others somewhere behind – only their squelching, panting and cursing to be heard.

At the side of that formidable wall a neatly uniformed sergeant-instructor (were his boots *really* shining?) began shouting. Dimly through the mental blur his words made sense: 'Sling your bloody rifles!' Automatically my head came down to pass through and allow the rifle to settle across my back. As I regained sight of Tim, my blood chilled.

He had already 'slung' his rifle. It was sailing twenty feet high over the wall, to the accompaniment of the outraged expletives of our father-figure the sergeant-instructor.

The rifle disappeared as we charged the obstacle, leaping vainly for a hand-hold and sliding futilely back down to collapse into the mire beneath. From the other side there came a grunt and a burst of light machine-gun fire. I caught a maniac gleam in Tim's eye as he boosted me to the top of the wall and I in turn heaved him up.

From there we enjoyed a grandstand view. The sergeant-instructor was tending an apparently unconscious corporal beside a drunkenly tilting Bren gun, mounted on a fixed tripod, and intended to fire across our next obstacle, the river.

It needed only a glance between us. We took our courage in both hands and fled, heading for the ice-cold river. Tim, on passing, retrieved his rifle from where it stood erect, barrel in the mud, like an ominous 1914/18 grave marker.

Two hundred yards shambling along between the red-tape course markers, and there was nowhere left to go but into the fast-flowing murky water of unknown depth. We landed in iced ooze up to the waist.

Another sergeant on the opposite bank was hollering at us to 'keep moving' upstream; as his shouts receded I vaguely heard something silly about keeping heads down when the Bren opened up.

Sure enough, round a curve there were big red flags. Even our stupefied minds knew what they meant, and as we approached, seeking the shallower water into the curve, from our left the Bren began to stutter quick bursts across the river.

The corporal could not have been badly hurt, but he must have been deeply offended. It would have been as patently obvious to him, as it was painfully apparent to us, that the Bren was off line and instead of firing horizontally four or five feet above the water, it was blasting down into the far bank.

At this juncture every sergeant-instructor and NCO (except

our mortified corporal who stuck manfully to his task and his lopsided Bren gun) arrived from miles around to oversee our discomfiture, exact revenge, and contribute unhelpful advice. All of which added up to a theory that if only we were neither so stunted, nor so illegitimate, and the water not too deep – or provided we were still capable of swimming, which definitely we were not – we could get through under the lee of the left bank where the river was fastest and deepest.

Cheered on by merry references to courts of inquiry, courts martial, the glasshouse, and bloody officer cadets, we lurched forward. The water reached my chin and I gained a sneaky satisfaction on seeing Tim, so much taller than I, crouch so low as we neared the line of fire that he, too, had to shut his mouth tight against the muddy stream.

Then that baptism of fire, the horrendous whip crack of every round passing what seemed like inches above our heads, until we were past and the Bren fell silent.

But not the pack of NCOs. Like hounds scenting a kill, they followed, anticipating something we did not.

On upstream we struggled, out of the river between the tapes, five hundred yards, reeling progress towards the firing range. At last a chance to lie down. But no rest. 'Load! Five rounds rapid! Fire!'

My first shot went off and for all I knew or cared it might have winged a crow in the far distance.

More hysterical shouts, more sergeants hopping dementedly up and down. Had I shot somebody?

A glance to my right. Poor Tim! It was most definitely not his day. He was staring in vague perplexity at his rifle barrel, open ended at the snout like a peeled banana skin. And as we dissolved into laughter I dimly remember Tim's voice: 'Sar'nt, shall I cease fire?'

At the subsequent court of inquiry, Tim was given a severe reprimand, and ordered to pay for the ruined Lee-Enfield. Officer material and a gentleman to the last, he asked the presiding officer whether he would take a cheque, and if so, could he borrow his pen?

But Seriously . . .

Earl Haig
Colditz POW Camp, 1944/45

I was one of the *Prominenten* (seven of us with connections with distinguished people in the UK) who were ordered by Hitler to be specially guarded, probably for future use as hostages. As things turned out the war ended too quickly for us to be used.

After arrival at Colditz, I was in a small cell with a table, chair and bed. Outside, the barred window was edged with white paint for ease of identification and, if necessary, marksmanship. I began to long for the company, even the coughing and talking, of my friends at Hadamar. Meanwhile, the guards marched stamping up and down the passage outside, stopping at intervals to peer through the spyhole in my door.

Through the small barred window of the cell I could see a sheer drop down the rock face with a series of barbed wire fences which lay between the castle and the woods beyond. The wire fences were covered by a number of watchtowers and wooden walkways which were patrolled by the guards. The whole scene was illuminated by searchlight and gave an eerie feeling, but mercifully we were spared this during our daily lives which were spent around the courtyard where guards were scarce, although quite large numbers of guards did emerge at times of appel or to carry out a search.

I was to spend three months in that cell, locked up ten hours a night, during a winter of extreme physical privation. The temperature fell to minus 15° Centigrade, and though there was a stove in the cell, the German ration of coal was too meagre to let me use it. During that time the supply of Red Cross parcels ceased. On my arrival our mess had to rely on its shrinking supply of reserve tins, but by Christmas these too had gone. The German rations were likewise cut down, so that we were living on a starvation diet – so low that the Germans themselves were anxious and weighed us all. These privations, coupled with an intense spiritual awareness which came partly from my work, and partly from anxiety about our future – and because I was sleeping monklike and alone – induced in me a heightened mental state akin to mysticism, so that as I lay awake my mind focused upwards along strange beams of light.

The Right Honourable Bernard Weatherill
Speaker of the House of Commons

With many who served in the Indian Army, I have never forgotten these words incribed on the wall of Chetwode Hall, The Indian Military Academy:

> The safety, honour and welfare of your country comes first – always and every time. The safety and comfort of the men you command comes next – always and every time. Your own safety and welfare comes last – always and every time.

★

'All of one Company = Fair Shares!'
When the British under Lord Nelson were bearing down upon the combined fleets at Trafalgar, the first lieutenant of *Revenge*, on going to check that all men were at their stations, observed the unusual sight of an old sailor on his knees by his gun. 'Are you afraid?' he asked.

'Afraid – certainly not.' 'I was only praying that the enemy shot would be distributed in the same proportion as the prize money – the greater part among the officers.'

People still expect fairness, not absolute fairness but reasonable fairness!

★

The best thing you can give your enemy is forgiveness.
The best thing you can give your opponent is tolerance.
The best thing you can give your friend is your heart.
The best thing you can give your father is deference.
The best thing you can give your mother is conduct that will make her proud of you.
The best thing you can give your child is a good example.
The best thing you can give yourself is respect.
The best thing you can give all men is charity.

Admiral Sir Guy Grantham

One night, during the evacuation of British and Commonwealth troops from Crete in 1941, my light cruiser, *Phoebe*, and destroyers were close in shore under the high hills at Spahkia on the south coast.

Soon after we had anchored, a Sunderland flying boat landed about two miles west of us, sent to embark General Freyberg, who had been ordered back to Egypt, with his staff.

At the same time to the east of us, the Germans were dropping parachute flares trying to find out whether embarkation was taking place on that stretch of the coast.

The general and staff needed the use of one of our two tank landing craft, which we could ill spare, and were using strong lights flashing in all directions. We were using no lights at all, and I thought the Sunderland's lights would inevitably draw the Germans' attention to what was going on further west of the area they were searching.

I was so angry, that I sent my executive officer in the fast sixteen-foot 'skimmer' to the Sunderland to tell the crew that if they did not douse all lights, except for take off, I would open fire on them with main armament. That was effective and we had no more trouble, and were not spotted by the Germans.

Major-General Sir John Acland

In 1979 a small commonwealth force, mainly British, of some 1500 men was sent to Rhodesia to attempt to bring peace between three armies, totalling some 60,000, undefeated in the field after seven years of bitter and bloody war – the two guerilla armies of Mr Mugabe and Mr Nkomo and that of the Rhodesian security forces.

The Commonwealth force went out in penny packets over a country the size of France, often on mined roads or, because of them, by RAF Hercules and helicopters, and into areas in which the Rhodesians had not operated for months, on a form of operation for which none had ever been trained. The Rhodesians said that these small parties of men, isolated and deep in the bush, faced certain death. They regarded the operation as suicidal.

Due, however, to the extraordinary courage of the young officers and soldiers who deployed, outstanding success was achieved and I believe that their courage was not one whit less than that of men who go into battle with the bullets flying. They had to face not just the unexpected but almost the unimaginable, with the likelihood of overwhelming odds against them; and their principal weapons not so much those they carried but willpower, self-control, humour and plain old-fashioned guts. One sign of fear, one faulty decision and the firing would have started and the operation would have failed.

That it succeeded speaks volumes for the calibre of the young men of today's services and it is as well that their predecessors from earlier and greater campaigns should know of it. Perhaps the message from the Governor, Lord Soames, sums it up:

Message from the Governor to Major-General John Acland for All Members of the Commonwealth Monitoring Force.

The task which you have been performing in Rhodesia is unique in the annals of military and political history.

From the military point of view, nobody has ever before even attempted what you have now achieved with such notable success. You have assured restraint and compliance with the ceasefire on the part of three undefeated armies still in the field after seven years of bitter war. The soldier's mission is peace; and in an unconventional fashion you have added a new page to the story of man's search for peace.

From the political point of view, you have made an indispensable contribution to what is also a unique exercise in government – turning a country from the paths of war to the holding of a democratic election within the space of three months.

This election makes possible a political solution to an otherwise intractable war. You have furnished a classic instance of the disciplined application of military capacity to a democratic political purpose.

On behalf of the people of Rhodesia I thank you for these signal services. The new state of Zimbabwe is being born under your sign. The members of the Commonwealth Monitoring Force are leaving a legacy to this new country – patience, understanding, courage and discipline. My thanks go out to you, together with the gratitude of countless people here and indeed throughout the world, for the healing touch you have brought to this land.

Date: *4 March 1980*   Signed: *Christopher Soames*

A. G. Palmer
Area Organizer, Eastern Area, The Royal British Legion

Many people are sceptical about fate playing a part in their life, but it certainly has in mine.

Firstly, I joined the Grenadier Guards for a period of seven years with the Colours, and five with the Reserve, in order that I might join the police force. However, whilst on leave from Palestine I was taken seriously ill and was discharged on medical grounds – but whilst in hospital I met and married my nurse.

Connections with the police were not severed as my brother and eldest son are both serving officers.

However, my mind goes back to the summer of 1946, when I was stationed at Victoria Barracks, Windsor. Entering the mess one afternoon, I noticed that extra tables had been erected and were covered with large white tablecloths.

Enquiring as to what was about to happen we discovered that two coachloads of disabled servicemen from Roehampton were dropping in for tea. Up to that point not much thought had ever been given to a disabled person, but to be faced with nearly one hundred, all with disabilities that meant they needed assistance, made one realize how lucky we were to have all our faculties.

In the party was a young double amputee whose stumps were insufficient to allow him to be fitted with artificial legs, but he was the life and soul of the party.

He was carried in by two guardsmen using a double-handed lift, and on his return to the coach was placed on the floor between the seats from whence he proceeded to hoist himself on to the seat.

Much backchat went to and fro on the coach and a remark was made from the rear of the coach to our legless friend with the result that he replied to the effect that, although he was unable to carry out the task as requested, he in turn could achieve something that no one else on the coach could do.

With a large grin on his face he proceeded to turn himself around on the seat quite easily and face the rear of the coach, a task impossible for a person with legs.

The courage and good humour of those men has remained with me ever since, a memory that has helped me during my Legion service at branch, group and county level, and more than ever in my present position as an area organizer.

Little did I realize in 1946, that nearly forty years on I would still be assisting many disabled ex-service men and women.

Was it fate that I should be in barracks on that particular day in 1946?

Index of Contributors

Index

The Royal British Legion

The sacrifices of Service men and women, as well as civilians, during two World Wars are well known. But few people are aware that, since the end of World War II, over 4000 British Service men and women have been killed on active service and more than 16,000 injured in some 70 so-called 'peacetime' conflicts, including the Falklands and today's tragedy in Northern Ireland.

The Royal British Legion is dedicated to honour the memory of those who died, and it not only helps the dependants of those killed, but also helps those ex-Service people whose lives have been shattered as a result of war. Amongst the ways in which the Legion helps the ex-Service community are the provision of work for disabled people; convalescent and residential care for the old and chronically sick; a free pensions advisory service; immediate aid during temporary or long-term illness, or when unemployment strikes; and the provision of holidays for the disabled. The Legion is particularly concerned with the plight of war widows and orphans.

To meet all our commitments, we need more than £7 million this year and so the Poppy Appeal is more crucial than ever before. The Legion urgently needs your support.

Please send a donation now to:

> Appeals Secretary
> The Royal British Legion
> Royal British Legion Village
> Maidstone
> Kent ME20 7NX
> Telephone: Maidstone (0622) 77172

If you would like more information on the Legion, or how to join this premier ex-Service organization with Branches and Clubs throughout the country, please write to:

> General Secretary
> The Royal British Legion
> 48 Pall Mall
> London SW1Y 5JY
> Telephone: 01-930 8131
> Registered Charity No. 225347